# *Musical* Elaborations

# Previously Published Wellek Library Lectures

# Edward W. Said

## *Musical* Elaborations

**THE WELLEK LIBRARY LECTURES**

at the University of California, Irvine

Columbia University Press ▪ New York

Columbia University Press

New York

Copyright © 1991 Edward W. Said

Library of Congress Cataloging-in-Publication Data

Said, Edward W.
  Musical elaborations / Edward W. Said.
    p.  cm.—(The Wellek library lectures at the Uni-
versity of California, Irvine)
  Includes bibliographical references and index.
  ISBN 0-231-07318-6
  1. Music—Philosophy and aesthetics.  2. Music and
society.  3. Music—Performance.  I. Title.  II. Series.
ML3845.S13  1991
781—dc20                                         90-26685
                                                      CIP
                    ⊗                                 MN

Casebound editions of Columbia University Press books
are printed on permanent and durable acid-free paper.

Acknowledgment is made to Boosey & Hawkes, Inc.,
for permission to quote extracts from Richard Strauss's
*Metamorphosen* (© 1946 by Boosey & Hawkes, Ltd.;
copyright renewed; reprinted by permission of Boosey
& Hawkes, Inc.) and from *Capriccio* (© copyright 1942
by Richard Strauss; copyright renewed; reprinted by
permission of Boosey & Hawkes, Inc., Publisher).

Printed in the United States of America

c 10 9 8 7 6 5 4 3 2

*To the memory of my mother*

To the memory of our mother

# Editorial Note

The Wellek Library Lectures in Critical Theory are given annually at the University of California, Irvine, under the auspices of the Critical Theory Institute. The following lectures were given in May 1989.

The Critical Theory Institute
Mark Poster, Director

# Contents

# Contents

# Acknowledgments

I am very grateful to Mark Poster who invited me to give these lectures at Irvine, and who very graciously offered me both hospitality and friendship. I'm also grateful to my old Irvine friends Homer Brown, John Rowe, and J. Hillis Miller, for their interest and support. Jon Weiner supplied me most generously with some good criticism and information. Fred Grab and Donald Mitchell gave me the benefit of their erudition, criticism, and friendship. Zaineb Istrabadi helped me a great deal in the preparation of the manuscript: her patience and competence were of invaluable importance. And Jennifer Crewe of Columbia University Press has been the most solicitous and helpful of editors.

My major, most painful regret is that—as the dedication of this book indicates—my mother died during its final preparation. It is to my mother's own wonderful musicality and love of the art that I owe my earliest interest in music. Over the years she has always been interested in my playing, and together we have shared many musical experiences together. I am more sorry than I can say that, regardless of its flaws, she did not live to read this book and tell me what she thought.

Edward W. Said
New York, July 7, 1990

# Introduction

When Professor Mark Poster of the University of California at Irvine invited me to give the 1989 Wellek Library Lectures in Critical Theory, he also suggested that I give them on a musical topic. I gladly accepted both of his invitations, of which this volume is one result.

I mention these circumstances because they have a lot to do with the nature of this book, for reasons I must immediately explain. In the first place, as three chapters that were originally three consecutive lectures, what I had to say benefited from a handsome setting (in the Irvine Faculty Club) and the facilities of modern communication. The room was well endowed not only with a good sound reproduction system, courtesy of the University's audiovisual department, but also with a fine grand piano. Many of my points and arguments were therefore illustrated either with recordings or, when I was unable to make my point as clearly or as sufficiently as I liked with a recording, with passages played on the piano. This immediacy, along with many of the improvised comments given rise to by the occasion, is partly lost in this printed version, although the text here is almost exactly the same as the lectures. Ideally it might have been possible to reproduce my musical examples on a cassette or disc attached to this volume, but for eminently practical reasons this turned out to have been prohibitively expensive and cumbersome. I have therefore resorted to printing extracts from musical texts, and in nearly every instance expanding my commentary about the extract to make up for the absence of direct musical performance.

In the second instance, this book is meant neither as a contribution to systematic musicology nor as a series of literary essays about music as it relates to literature (the latter is my principal field of knowledge). Rather I have tried to discuss three aspects of Western classical music from the standpoint of someone who has had much to do with music and who over the years has been thinking about music in many of the same ways made possible by contemporary thought about literature. Music, like literature, is practiced in a social and cultural setting, but it is also an art whose existence is premised undeniably on individual performance, reception, or production. Perhaps I only speak for myself when I say that in the end actually *playing* the music is what gives one the most satisfaction and pleasure, and yet of course we are able to play (or compose) because of a huge variety of other factors, many of them social and historical. I have therefore found myself in this book trying to be as conscious as possible on the one hand of the ideal purity of the individual experience, and on the other, of its public setting, even when music is most inward, most private.

The large literature that exists on music deals with these two poles and much that lies between them, in all sorts of interesting ways, many of which have helped me a great deal. But I agree with Joseph Kerman in *Contemplating Music: Challenges to Musicology* that much of this work is basically "positivistic" (he quotes Donald Mitchell on this point) and, I would add, reverential. There are certainly new critical trends—among which Kerman most approvingly cites Charles Rosen's *The Classical Style*—but to an outsider from an adjacent humanistic field these trends, and even Rosen himself, seem not to have kept pace with many of the great advances made in other branches of humanistic interpretation.[1] This is a matter neither of trendiness nor of critical orthodoxy and jargon. We *do* know more about the way cultures operate thanks to Raymond Williams, Roland Barthes, Michel Foucault, and Stuart Hall; we know about how to examine a text in ways that Jacques Derrida, Hayden White, Fredric Jameson, and Stanley Fish have significantly expanded and altered; and thanks to feminists like Elaine Showalter, Germaine Greer, Hélène Cixous, Sandra Gilbert, Susan Gubar, and Gayatri Spivak it is impossible to avoid or ignore the gender issues in the production and interpretation of art.

There has always been a healthy interchange between writing music or about music and general interpretive theory. To speak only of nineteenth century composers, Beethoven and the Enlightenment, or Wagner and Schopenhauer, is a relatively straightforward relationship based on avowed influence or indebtedness. But I think that if we leave aside a certain basic level of technical musical analysis (up to and including Schenkerian analysis) the most interesting, the most valuable, and the most distinguished modern writing about music is, to use Edward Cone's phrase, writing that self-consciously sees itself as a "humanistic discipline." Maynard Solomon on Beethoven, Winton Dean on Handel, Donald Mitchell on Mahler, Vladimir Jankélévitch on Fauré, Paul Griffiths on Messaien: these fine writers come immediately to mind as exemplars of the sort of work Cone has in mind, with truly impressive results that are of interest both to the specialist and to the general culturally informed reader. If we add names like those of Kerman himself, Cone, Leonard Meyer, Richard Taruskin, Philip Gossett, Leo Treitler, Wilfrid Mellers, the philosopher Peter Kivy, cultural historians Paul Robinson and Herbert Lindenberger, we will have before us modern humanistic and critical scholarship on music at its very best.

Nevertheless, few of the excellent musicological scholars in

1. See the penetrating review of Kerman's book by Christopher Gibbs, in *Current Musicology* 39 (1985): 66–74.

this group write about music as, say, Williams wrote about literature, or Foucault about the history of disciplines. Lindenberger and Robinson stand out, I think, because they operate outside musicology. This is not at all to denigrate what musicologists do, or to suggest that in some generally *chic* way they are not progressive enough. It is to say, however, that because music's autonomy from the social world has been taken for granted for at least a century, and because the technical requirements imposed by musical analysis are so separate and severe, there is a putative, or ascribed, fullness to self-sufficient musicological work that is now much less justified than ever before. When even the most hermetic and specialized writers like Joyce or Mallarmé are accessible to ideological or psychoanalytic analysis of a far from crudely reductionist kind, there is no reason to exclude music from similar scrutiny.

The point I am making is that the study of music can be more, and not less, interesting if we situate music as taking place, so to speak, in a social and cultural setting. Another way of putting this is to say that the *roles* played by music in Western society are extraordinarily varied, and far exceed the antiseptic, cloistered, academic, professional aloofness it seems to have been accorded. Think of the affiliation between music and social privilege; or between music and the nation; or between music and religious veneration—and the idea will be clear enough. The difficulty, however, is to devise modes of articulating musical activity in that larger context, a difficulty only just beginning to be approached systematically.

Younger scholars of music like Rose Subotnik, Carolyn Abbate, Jeffrey Kahlberg, Susan McClary—to name only a very few—have already started to avail themselves, without any loss in musical accuracy or scholarship, of what deconstruction, cultural history, narratology, and feminist theory have to offer. But for all its brilliance, their work is both at a relatively early stage and, I have gathered, occupies minority if not marginal status in musicology. True, things are changing, but, in the main, professional musicology is like any other field in that it has a corporate or guild consensus to maintain, which sometimes requires keeping things as they are, not admitting new or outlandish ideas, maintaining boundaries and enclosures. And while I am very far indeed from rejecting all, or even a significant portion, of what musicologists do by way of analysis or evaluation, I am struck by how much does not receive their critical attention, and by how little is actually done by fine scholars who, for example, in studying a composer's notebooks or the structure of classical form, fail to connect those things to ideology, or social space, or power, or to the formation of an individual (and by no means sovereign) ego.

Theodor Adorno may have been the last thinker about Western classical music to attempt many of these bigger things. I have little idea what his influence or status is in musicology today but I suspect that his intransigent theorizing, complicated philosophical language, and vast speculative pessimism do not endear him to busy professionals. His disciple Carl Dahlhaus carried on in Adorno's line with much more coverage and visibility to show for it than Adorno, but even with Dahlhaus's *oeuvre* (as a long recent survey of his work by Philip Gossett in *The New York Review of Books* attests)[2] there is a tendency for other musicologists to pick at Adorno's weaknesses rather than to confront his postulations or emulate the theoretical breadth and magisterial scope of his best work.

Understandably then it must fall to rank outsiders with no professional musicological reputation at stake to venture the risky, often impressionistic theorizing and descriptions that this book puts forward. It bears repeating that I am not carrying on *against* musicology in these pages. Instead my primary interest is to look at Western classical music as a cultural field that has meant a great deal to me as literary critic and musician, and to see in it issues and formations that are especially worthy of attention to students of the best in contemporary cultural studies.

2. In the issue of October 26, 1989 (Vol. 36, #16).

Not surprisingly I have found myself debating Adorno some of the time. His dark renderings of the current musical scene are based on ideas and *aperçus* that are completely different from mine, for reasons having to do with his European background and his age. Most of his best work was done in the years immediately prior to World War II, and in its aftermath. My largely American education was entirely completed well after the war, and my non-Western background has not allowed me to assume many of the values and teleologies he takes for granted. But like Adorno—and perhaps with as little justification—I accept the existence of a relatively distinct entity called "Western classical music," although at a later occasion perhaps I'd like to show that it is far from coherent or monolithic and that when it is talked about as if it meant only one thing it is being constructed with non-Western, nonclassical musics and cultures very much in mind. Nevertheless, Adorno gives one plenty to think about, particularly when he presents a dramatic trajectory for music that begins in the late compositions of Beethoven and moves through Wagner to the Second Viennese school, and finally comes to rest (in the words of a stunning essay of his) during the period when "new music grows old." In addition I have been provoked by Adorno's ideas about the regression of listening, and of course by his melodramatic association of music with the German catastrophe under fascism.

In arguing with him here and there I have actually, I believe, been either extending or changing his premises somewhat to suit mine. Adorno is a creature of the Hegelian tradition, which presumes an inescapable historical teleology that incorporates everything in its relentless forward path. This I find unacceptable for all sorts of reasons. Rather than spelling them out here I shall briefly suggest an alternative based on a *geographical* or spatial idea that is truer to the diversity and spread of human activity. Even if we confine ourselves to "Western" classical music, what is impressive about musical practice in all its variety is that it takes place in many different places, for different purposes, for different constituencies and practitioners, and of course at many different times. To assemble all that, to herd it under one dialectical temporal model is—no matter how compelling or dramatic the formulation—simply an untrue and therefore insufficient account of what happens.

Moreover, classical music participates in the differentiation of social space, its elaboration if you will. The late twentieth-century concert hall, for example, shares some things in common with the museum and the library, but because concert music unfolds in a highly rarified temporal duration, *performance* is therefore of greater immediate import—more urgent, more stressed and inflected—for music than it is for the reception of either literature or painting. One can reread a book, or revisit an exhibition: it makes no sense to "revisit" a concert, although recordings have changed that fact considerably. In any event, as I try to show in Chapter One, concert occasions are always located in a uniquely endowed site, and what occurs then and there is part of the cultural life of modern society.

Some of the ideological meaning embedded in scenarios of what happened to "the West" during World War II and its immediate aftermath constitutes the starting point for Chapter Two, "On the Transgressive Elements in Music." What supervenes thereafter is the consciousness of a non-Westerner, for whom the remorseless totalizing to be found both in Adorno and in Thomas Mann's *Doctor Faustus* is an instigation for thinking about *alternative* patterns. Far from denying music's unique magic, however, I have capitalized on it, finding it almost routinely associated with and sought out by various authorities and patrons in civil society—court, church, and so forth. What I mean by "transgression" is something completely literal and secular at the same time: that faculty music has to travel, cross over, drift from place to place in a society, even though many institutions and orthodoxies have sought to confine it. I take a romantic view nonetheless in arguing finally that music to a consummate musician possesses a separate status and place (echoes of Schubert's "An die Musik" come to my aid here) that is occasionally revealed but more often with-held.

Thus during the period from the seventeenth century on, music for the most part plays a role in what Antonio Gramsci has called the conquest of civil society. As Susan McClary once suggested to me, this is the import of some recent works: by Gary Tomlinson, in his *Monteverdi and the End of the Renaissance,* and by Lorenzo Bianconi, in his *Music in the Seventeenth Century.* There are descriptions of this kind of musical elaboration in other works that I discuss elsewhere in this book, but I shouldn't leave the impression that there is only one hege-mony, one orthodoxy, and one social authority to which music has affixed itself opportunistically. On the contrary, Western classical music is a much contested thing, with all sorts of establishments, heterodoxies, upstarts, and challengers vying for the attention and prominence that come with "having" music. I have not been able to discuss in any detail this rather more sporty aspect of my subject in this book, but it has been one of my main concerns in the musical columns I have written for *The Nation* since 1986. Why, for instance, has Chopin, who is a tremendously advanced and gifted composer, been margin-alized as an effeminate salon decoration; why has the Austro-Germanic symphonic tradition crowded out Czech, French, or Spanish composers; and why has a deadly combination of text-book naturalism and *verismo* idioms nearly completely domi-nated American opera performance style and repertory in places like the Metropolitan?

No less interesting is the role played by music in the various dissenting alternatives to the social mainstream. I refer to that in my analysis of Wagner, but alas, there too my mapping and surveying is more cursory than I would have liked and needs supplementing. Yet in my final chapter I do treat one such alternative, which I associate with what I call solitude, mem-ory, and affirmation. This, I think, is where I separate most definitively from Adorno, for whom in the totally administered society no person is exempt from ideological coercion. No one can disagree with his contention that packaging, commodification, reification—the whole list—have overtaken much of what is happiest, most fulfilling about the art of music. Pleasure and privacy do remain, however, and it is an investigation of this, with Proust as my guide, that brings this book to a conclusion. For, I believe, *not all* music can be experienced as working toward domination and sovereignty, just as not all music follows the awesomely invigorating patterns of sonata form. As to whether in the end I propose either a utopian or an idealistic mode, I can't really say, except to insist that in a literal sense it is the view of a fully committed *amateur*, which is not so disabling a status as one might think.

# Performance as an
# Extreme Occasion

One of the significant statements in contemporary literary criticism occurs at the opening of Richard Poirier's classic essay "The Performing Self." He is discussing modern writers like Yeats, Norman Mailer, and Henry James whose "powers of rendition" define the "performance that matters—pacing, economics, juxtapositions, aggregations of tone, the whole conduct of the shaping presence." And if this, says Poirier, partakes of brutality and even savagery it is because

> Performance is an exercise of power, a very anxious one. Curious because it is at first so furiously self-consultive, so even narcissistic, and later so eager for publicity, love and historical dimensions. Out of an accumulation of secretive acts emerges at last a form that presumes to compete with reality itself for control of the mind exposed to it. Performance in writing, in painting, or in dance is made of thousands of tiny movements each made with a calculation that is also its innocence. By innocence I mean that the movements have an utterly moral neutrality–they are designed to serve one another and nothing else; and they are innocent, too, because contrived with only a vague general notion of

what they might ultimately be responsible for—the final thing, the accumulation called "the work."[1]

Poirier's purpose in these lines is to separate the academic, liberal, and melioristic attitudes toward literature, attitudes that serve codes, institutions, and orthodoxies, from the processes of literary performance that, he argues, are essentially "dislocating, disturbing impulses." Yet performance is not merely a happening but rather "an action which must go through passages that both impede the action and give it form." Thus, "performance comes to function at precisely the point where the potentially destructive impulse to mastery brings forth from the material its most essential irreducible, clarified, and therefore beautiful nature."[2]

Although Poirier does not discuss music here, all of his comments about rendition and enactment—except perhaps the one about innocence, to which I'd like to return later—are deeply pertinent to modern musical performance, which is also rather like an athletic event in its demand for the admiringly rapt attention of its spectators. Yet Poirier's literary examples are drawn from the work of creative artists, whereas the performances that concern me here are the essentially re-creative and interpretive reenactments of musical compositions by pianists, violinists, singers, and so forth. Indeed we should begin by noting how the extreme specialization of all aesthetic activity in the contemporary West has overtaken and been inscribed within musical performance so effectively as to screen entirely the composer from the performer. There are no major performers before the public today who are also influential composers of the first rank; even Pierre Boulez and Leonard Bernstein, to mention two immediately obvious possible exceptions, belong separately albeit simultaneously and equally to the worlds of composing and of performing, but it is not as performers of

1. Richard Poirier, *The Performing Self: Compositions and Decompositions in the Languages of Contemporary Life* (New York: Oxford University Press, 1971), p. 87.
2. *Ibid.*, p. xiv.

their own work that they are known principally. Beethoven, Mozart, Chopin, and Liszt were.

There is a further specialization to be noted, that of the listeners or spectators who in the aggregate make up audiences at events of musical performance. Some years ago Adorno wrote a famous and, I think, correct account of "the regression of hearing," in which he emphasized the lack of continuity, concentration, and knowledge in the listeners that has made real musical attention more or less impossible. Adorno blamed such things as radio and records for undermining and practically eliminating the possibility that the average concertgoer could play an instrument or read a score.[3] To those disabilities we can add today's complete professionalization of performance. This has widened the distance between the "artist" in evening dress or tails and, in a lesser, lower, far more secondary space, the listener who buys records, frequents concert halls, and is routinely made to feel the impossibility of attaining the packaged virtuosity of a professional performer. Whether we focus on the repeatable mechanically reproduced performance available on disc, tape, or video-record, or on the alienating social ritual of the concert itself, with the scarcity of tickets and the staggeringly brilliant technique of the performer achieving roughly the same distancing effect, the listener is in a relatively weak and not entirely admirable position. Here Poirier's rather melodramatic ideas about brutality, savagery, and power can be moderated with an acknowledgment of the listener's poignant speechlessness as he/she faces an onslaught of such refinement, articulation, and technique as almost to constitute a sadomasochistic experience.[4]

Consider as an example the performance of Chopin's Etudes by Maurizio Pollini, the extraordinarily proficient and brilliant Italian pianist. His interpretation is available on disc and, since

3. Theodor W. Adorno, "On the Fetish Character in Music and the Regression of Listening" (1938), in *The Essential Frankfurt School Reader*, ed. Andrew Arato and Eike Gebhardt (New York: Urizen Books, 1978), especially pp. 286–99.
4. I have discussed this in *The Nation*, December 25, 1989, pp. 802–4.

Pollini performs the works regularly in recital and was also winner of the Chopin Prize when he was only eighteen, these recorded performances of opus 10 and opus 25 stand as representative of his considerable virtuosity. Chopin wrote them originally as aids to his teaching, as explanations of various aspects of keyboard technique (octaves, thirds, left-hand and passage work, legato playing, arpeggios, etc.). In Pollini's performance the power and astonishing assertiveness of the playing, which begins in opus 10, number 1, with a massive C-major bass octave chord and is immediately followed by a burst of lightning-fast arpeggiated passage work, absolutely free of hesitation, wrong notes, or grasping, immediately establishes the distance between these performances and any amateur attempt to render Chopin's music. Moreover, the grandeur of Pollini's technique, its scale, and its dominating display and reach completely dispatch any remnant of Chopin's original intention for the music, which was to afford the pianist, any pianist, an entry into the relative seclusion and reflectiveness of problems of technique.

Evidence testifying to the performer's power, unattached to the correlative skills either of improvisation or of composing, emerges after the first third of the nineteenth century. The virtuoso singer, pianist, or violinist who is the ancestor of today's Jessye Norman, Pollini, or Menuhin comes not just with the appearance of Paganini on European stages in the late 1820s, the great archetype of the preternaturally skilled and demonic performer on endlessly fascinating display, but with the emergence of transcription as an art both of display and of encroachment, and along with transcription a relative demotion in the priority of the musical text (about which in his magisterial book *Nineteenth Century Music* Carl Dahlhaus has interesting things to say).[5] When pianists invade the orchestral or operatic repertoire we have gone well beyond even the contests in virtuosity that engaged Bach, Handel, and Mozart,

5. Carl Dahlhaus, *Nineteenth Century Music*, trans. J. Bradford Robinson (Berkeley: University of California Press, 1989), especially pp. 137–42.

who played the music of other masters as easily as they canni-
balized and plagiarized their own work. Modern performance
has to do with rights asserted over music written by and for
others, rights won by a rigorous, highly specialized training in
interpretation most often not grounded in composition. Busoni
may be the last of the major còmposers, transcribers, and performers to operate before a Western musical public; the line of
impressive omni-competent musicians that was so boldly begun with Bach, so robustly continued with Beethoven, so color-
fully overstated with Liszt and Busoni, disappears completely
after Rachmaninoff, Prokofiev, Britten, and Bartok.

Performance cut off from composing therefore constitutes a
special form of ownership and work. Let me return briefly to
transcription, since it is in the theory and practice of transcription that the various incorporations and consolidations of mo-
nopolistic performance most strikingly take place. There is in
all Western classical music from the late seventeenth century
on a dynamic between performance designed for the public
place secured and held by church and court, on the one hand,
and, on the other hand, music whose performance is private
and domestic. Orchestral and choral works of any moderate
size belong principally to the public sphere, although both Bach
and Handel trafficked across the lines so to speak in writing
music that could be performed in either one space or the other,
by one kind of instrument, solo or concerted, or another. Many
of Beethoven's instrumental works and lieder were written for
nonprofessionals, although they have since become standard
works in the performing repertory of professional singers and
instrumentalists.

The main nineteenth-century examples of transcription were
(and have remained in the twentieth century) the reductions of
large concerted works to the smaller resources of one instrument, most often the piano. This practice argues the steady
presence of amateur musicians who could not readily obtain or
decipher full scores but whose desire to play the music could
be satisfied by reading and playing it in piano versions for

either two or four hands. Before records and radio this in fact was the main introduction to concert music for uncounted numbers of people for whom—even after mechanical reproduction became a standard feature of modern life—the pleasure of getting control of a full score, and enacting a concert event in the home, was perhaps greater and certainly more frequent than attending concerts. The transcription for public concert purposes of operas, of music for other instruments (especially the organ) and for voice, as well as of full-scale orchestral works, is a qualitatively different thing, however. Liszt was the most famous exemplar of this practice, which at last enters the public sphere in the 1840s and makes a new kind of statement about the act of performance itself.

At the simplest level, Liszt's transcriptions are an art of sustained and extended quotation, and later of quotation prolonged elaborately into what Liszt was to call a concert paraphrase or fantasia. The variations, paraphrases, fantasias he wrote on Bach's "Weinen, Klagen, Sorgen, Zagen" and on Verdi's *Rigoletto* are well-known examples that still turn up on contemporary recital programs. But on a second level, concert quotations that became full-fledged pieces on their own, autonomous works that leave behind the original or blot it out entirely, are assertions of the transcriber's skill and, much more important, of the performer's virtuosity. For not only does the listener marvel (as people marveled at Liszt's fastidious transcription of the Beethoven Sixth Symphony) at how only a magician could reduce and render a full score so idiomatically for the piano, but the work's formidable digital difficulty is a display of the concert musician's prerogative to help her/himself to pieces from the repertory of orchestra, organ, or opera and establish them in a new, highly specialized environment.

With his considerably advanced and almost metacritical sense of what the performer's work was really about, Glenn Gould illustrated the main features of this new environment as it had developed by the mid-twentieth century. Consider as a start that he was the first major performer to announce his retire-

ment from the concert stage at age thirty-one; he then pro-
ceeded to spend the rest of his life publicly saying that he had
done so, all the while performing around, but never again in,
the concert hall. He made dozens of recordings, wrote numerous articles, lectured, did radio and television work, and acted
as producer for many of his own performances. Second, no
sooner had he deserted concert life than Gould's repertory
suddenly departed from the mainly Baroque and contemporary
works in which he excelled and for which he had become
famous. He began a new career as "concert-dropout" playing
not just Bach and Schoenberg but Liszt's piano transcriptions
of the Beethoven Fifth and Sixth symphonies; in a later recording he delivered himself of his own transcriptions of Wagner,
including "Dawn and Rhine Journey" from *Götterdämmerung* as
well as the Prelude to *Die Meistersinger*. So complicated and
intimidatingly difficult were these scores that Gould's point
seemed to be that he wanted to reassert the pianist's prerogative to dominate over all other fields of music, and to do so
completely as a function of unapproachably superior, uniquely
"different" capacities for instrumental display.

There is even a dramatic point being underscored in the
actual reduction of score from its full orchestral version, which
is what Beethoven wrote, to its brilliant pianistic miniaturiza-
tion by Liszt. To see the difference in size between the two
versions is to note that the piano reduction is the metaphoric
equivalent of forcing an army to walk single-file through a
single turnstyle, with the pianist as gatekeeper (Example 1 and
Example 2).

Only a professional pianist can render such a work as this—
here we must note how pianists play the preeminent role in the
developments I am describing—just as the act of executing
such a work is no longer an act of affection (*amateur* is a word
to be taken first in its literal sense) but an act of almost institu-
tional mastery and therefore a public occasion. Similarly the
sheer length and the scope of the solo performance in the
nineteenth century transcriptions were designed for the tech-

EXAMPLE 1. Beethoven's Symphony No. 5 in C Minor, opening of first movement

EXAMPLE 2. Liszt's piano transcription of Example 1

nical virtuosity—the complex chordal and passage work, leaps, etc., that had emerged as the hallmark of piano playing after Beethoven—of the performer's actual playing. What today we experience in the concert hall is the completed relocation of the site of a score's musical realization from the amateur's home to the concert hall, from an ordinary, mainly domestic and private passage of time, to an occasional, heightened public experience of the solo or concert repertory by a professional performer.

After the middle of the nineteenth century virtuosos seem to have regarded their concerts not just as samplings of a few works (that practice continues today) but as marathon surveys of the entire musical literature. And indeed, in the legendary programs put on by Busoni in Berlin and by Anton Rubinstein in St. Petersburg, audiences got immense multi-hour traversals of the whole keyboard repertory. Attenuated versions of these recitals continue today in the all-Beethoven cycles executed by Artur Schnabel, Alfred Brendel, Daniel Barenboim, and Richard Goode, among others. The great master professionals become in fact the living embodiment of their instrument's history, their programs the narrative of that history presented didactically and integrally. The celebrated orchestral conductors attempt a similar combination of performance and history (Bernstein and the Mahler symphonies, Karajan and the Bruckner symphonies, Solti and Wagner, Toscanini and Beethoven).

Until the early twentieth century most concert performers who were not composers routinely scheduled the work of contemporary composers on their program. Artur Rubinstein was probably the last pianist a significant portion of whose repertory until he died a few years ago was made up of works (the Stravinsky *Petrushka*, Ravel's *Valses Nobles et Sentimentales*, many pieces by Szymanowski, Albeniz, de Falla) he played as their composers' contemporary and friend. But this practice has fallen off dramatically. Ursula Oppens, a fine New York pianist, is one of the few first-rate professionals still doing that. Otherwise the concert professional's programs are if not antiquarian, then curatorial, with occasional nods at the musician's obligation also to be instructive and acceptably contemporary.

Performances of Western classical music are therefore highly concentrated, rarified, and extreme occasions. They have a commercial rationale that is connected not just to selling tickets and booking tours but also to selling records for the benefit of large corporations. Above all, the concert occasion itself is the result of a complex historical and social process—some aspects of which I have tried to present here—that can be interpreted as a cultural occasion staked upon specialized eccentric skills, upon the performer's interpretive and histrionic personality fenced in by his or her obligatory muteness, upon the audience's receptivity, subordination, and paying patience. What competes with these occasions is not the amateur's experience but other public displays of specialized skill (sports, circus, dance contests) that, at its worst and most vulgar, the concert may attempt to match.

What interests me about the concert occasion is what interests me in all the musical topics I have chosen for discussion here, namely, that there is an enduring perhaps even atavistic quality to certain aspects of the performance, interpretation, and production of Western classical music that can be studied and examined precisely because the integrity and specialization involved nevertheless converge upon other cultural and theoretical issues that are not musical, or that do not belong completely to the sphere of music. Clearly, for example, musical performance, with its narcissistic, self-referential, and, as Poirier says, self-consultive qualities, is the central and most socially stressed musical experience in modern Western society, but it is both a private musical experience for performer and listener, and a public experience too. The two experiences are interdependent and overlap with each other. But how can one understand the connection between the two and, more interestingly, how does one interpret it? Are there particularly useful ways of doing so in order that the enabling conditions of performance and their connection with the sociocultural sphere can be seen as a coherent part of the whole experience?

Now the connection between modern or new music and contemporary Western society has been the subject of Theodor Adorno's extremely influential theoretical reflections and analysis. There are three things, however, about Adorno's work that in a sense start me off here, and from which, for reasons I shall explain briefly, I necessarily depart. The first is Adorno's theory that after Beethoven (who died in 1827) music veered off from the social realm into the aesthetic almost completely. According to Adorno, Beethoven's late style gains for music a new autonomy from the world of ordinary historical reality.[6] Adorno believed that it was Arnold Schoenberg's extraordinary achievement in his theory and career a hundred years after Beethoven's death to have first comprehended and subsumed the real meaning of music's trajectory in the preceding century, and then having thoroughly incorporated it, to have derived

6. Adorno, "Spätstil Beethovens" (1937), in *Gesammelte Schriften 17* (Frankfurt: Suhrkamp, 1982), pp. 13–17. By far the best English-language account of the significance of Adorno's views is to be found in Rose R. Subotnik, "Adorno's Diagnosis of Beethoven's Late Style: Early Symptoms of Fatal Condition," *Journal of the American Musicological Society* 29 (Summer 1976): 251–53.

his new rationale from a deepened, tragic intensification of the separation between music and society.[7]

The technicalization of the dodecaphonic system, its totally rationalized form and preprogrammed expressiveness, its forcefully articulated laws, are an elimination of transcendence and an affirmation and alienation as well; everything about music that had characterized it hitherto, its concepts of improvisation, creativity, composition, variation, and sociability, now come, Adorno says, to a paralyzed standstill.[8] From the time of the Baroque, music had been not only a documentation of the bourgeoisie's reality but also one of its principal art forms, since the proletariat never formulated or was permitted to constitute itself as a musical subject. By the early twentieth century, radical modern music of the kind composed by Schoenberg and his main disciples Berg and Webern has had its social substance abstracted from it by entirely musical means. New music has become isolated and hermetic not by virtue of "asocial" but rather because of social concerns.

Thus modern music expresses its social "concern through its pure quality, doing so all the more emphatically, the more purely this quality is revealed; it points out the ills of society rather than sublimating those ills into a deceptive humanitarianism which would pretend that humanitarianism had already been achieved in the present." Adorno continues: "The alienation present in the consistency of artistic technique forms the very substance of the work of art. The shocks of incomprehension, emitted by artistic technique, undergo a sudden change. They illuminate the meaningless world."[9] I take Adorno to be saying that by its very rigor and distance from the everyday world of listeners and perhaps even of performers, new music

7. This is the theme of Adorno's *Philosphie der neuen Musik* (1949), whose English translation is *Philosophy of Modern Music*, trans. Anne G. Mitchell and Wesley V. Blomster (New York: Seabury Press, 1973). The book depends allusively on Adorno's conceptions of late Beethoven and Wagner.

8. Adorno, *Philosophy of Modern Music*, p. 102.

9. *Ibid.*, p. 131.

casts a devastatingly critical light upon the degraded and there-fore meaningless world, precisely the world for which Georg Lukács thirty years before in *The Theory of the Novel* had de-signed his interpretation of the form of the novel.

"Modern music," Adorno concludes,

> sacrifices itself to this effort. It has taken upon itself all the darkness and guilt of the world. Its fortune lies in the percep-tion of misfortune; all of its beauty is in denying itself the illusion of beauty. No one wished to become involved with art—individuals as little as collectives. It dies away unheard, without even an echo. . . . Music which has not been heard falls into empty time like an impotent bullet. Modern music spontaneously aims towards this last experience, evidenced hourly in mechanical [by which Adorno means music that is reproduced mechanically, unthinkingly, like Muzak or back-ground music] means. Modern music sees absolute oblivion as its goal. It is the surviving message of despair from the shipwrecked.[10]

The commanding figure of Schoenberg dominates and gloomily irradiates this description but, I believe, most of what Adorno theorizes about turns out to have little prophetic validity, aside from its rather willful avoidance of such "new" composers as Debussy, Busoni, and Janácek. (To his credit he wrote an essay years later entitled "Modern Music Is Growing Old" conceding the point.)[11] Not only did serialism become an academic, thor-oughly (too) respectable technique but many of the early mas-terpieces of the Viennese twelve-tone method are now items of considerable prestige and frequency in the performing reper-tory.

Some of the alienating distance of the ascetic compositional techniques described so powerfully by Adorno nevertheless survives in the rituals of virtuoso performance that, despite the

---

10. *Ibid.*, p. 133.

11. Adorno's thesis is that, whereas for Schoenberg the twelve-tone system was the enactment of a historical and philosophical crisis, for today's component it has lost its urgency entirely. "Modern Music Is Growing Old," *The Score* 18 (De-cember 1956): 18–29.

relative scarcity of virtuosity, nevertheless continue into the present. Classical music is not only not unheard but is heard in new configurations of aesthetic and social experience. Thus what furnished us with an excellent starting point—the observation that Adorno's characterization of new music is true for the period during which he wrote—is inadequate once we are past the period of the Second Viennese school's apogee in the 1920s; analysis must be extended into a present to which the application of Adorno's prescriptive admonishments appears (dare one say it?) sentimental. The fact is that music remains situated within the social context as a special variety of aesthetic and cultural experience that contributes to what, following Gramsci, we might call the elaboration or production of civil society. In Gramsci's usage elaboration equals maintenance, that is, the work done by members of a society that keeps things going; certainly musical performance fits the description, as do cultural activities like lectures, conferences, graduation ceremonies, awards banquets, etc. The problematics of great musical performance, social as well as technical, therefore provide us with a post-Adornian occasion for analysis and for reflecting on the role of classical music in contemporary Western society.

My second point about Adorno, to whose work I am profoundly indebted in all sorts of ways, is illuminated by an anecdote recounted by Pierre Boulez on the occasion of Michel Foucault's death. Although he and Foucault never spoke about their intellectual specialties to each other—Foucault about philosophy, Boulez about composition—it transpired that Foucault once noted to Boulez the remarkable ignorance of contemporary intellectuals about music, whether classical or popular.[12] Perhaps the two men had in mind the contrast with a previous generation of European intellectuals for whom reflection on music was a central part of their work. Certainly Adorno and Ernst Bloch, for example, demonstrate in their careers the strik-

12. "Quelques souvenirs de Pierre Boulez," *Critique* 471–72 (Août-Septembre 1986): 745–47.

ing relevance of, say, philosophy and religion to music, or the intrinsically necessary presence of musical analysis to Adorno's negative dialectics or Bloch's theses on hope and utopian thought.

As we look back to the modernist movement for which music was culturally central—Proust, Mann, Eliot, Joyce come additionally to mind—we have good reason to remark that just as Adorno was able to rationalize and ironically connect Schoenberg's work in and for modern society, we are able to demonstrate how in the general division of intellectual labor after modernism musical experience was fragmented. Historical musicology, theory, ethnomusicology, composition today furnish most academic music departments with four distinct enterprises. For its part, music criticism is now effectively the report of attendance at concerts that are really evanescent happenings, unrepeatable, usually unrecordable, nonrecuperable. And yet in the interesting recharting of intellectual undertakings attempted by what has been called cultural studies, certain aspects of the musical experience can be understood inclusively as taking place within the cultural setting of the contemporary West.[13] The performance occasion, as I have been calling it, is one such aspect, which is why I shall be looking at it from this broad cultural perspective.

Lastly, Adorno's main argument about modern music is that its exclusivism and hermetic austerity do not constitute something new but testify rather to a quasi-neurotic insistence on music's separate, almost mute, and formally nondiscursive character as an art. Anyone who has written or thought about music has of course confronted the problem of meaning and interpretation, but must always return to a serious appraisal of how music manages in spite of everything to preserve its reticence, mystery, or allusive silence, which in turn symbolizes its autonomy as an art. The Adornian model for music history as compellingly analyzed by Rose Subotnik suggests that music

13. A perspicacious example is Alan Durant's *Conditions of Music* (London: Macmillan, 1984).

eludes philosophical statement only after Beethoven, and that the "alienation present in the consistency of [Schoenberg's] musical technique" is a fulfillment of the privatization of the art begun during the early days of romanticism.[14] I do not disagree with this view, nor it would seem does Carl Dahlhaus, whose monumental study *Nineteenth Century Music* (referred to earlier) fleshes out the same model with considerable subtlety and detail. But it *is*, I think, accurate to say that we can regard the public nature of musical performance today—professionalized, ritualized, specialized though it may be—as a way of bridging the gap between the social and cultural spheres on the one hand, and music's reclusiveness on the other. Performance is thus an inflected and highly determined point of convergence where the specific and the general come together, music as the most specialized of aesthetics with a discipline entirely specific to it, performance as the general, socially available form of its cultural presentation.

Yet—and here I return now to my main argument about performance as an occasion—it is appropriate to stress the social abnormality of the concert ritual itself. What attracts audiences to concerts is that what performers attempt on the concert or opera stage is exactly what most members of the audience cannot emulate or aspire to. But this unattainable actuality, so strikingly dramatic when we see it before us on a stage, depends on the existence of unseen faculties and powers that make it possible: the performers' training and gifts; cultural agencies like concert associations, managers, ticketsellers; the conjunction of various social and cultural processes (including the revolutions in capitalism and telecommunication, electronic media, jet travel) with an audience's wish or appetite for a particular musical event. The result is what can be called an extreme occasion, something beyond the everyday, something irreducibly and temporally not repeatable, something whose

---

14. Subotnik, "The Historical Structure: Adorno's 'French' Model for the Criticism of Nineteenth-Century Music," *19th Century Music* 2 (July 1978): 36–60.

core is precisely what can be experienced only under relatively severe and unyielding conditions.

At no point has the extremism and severity of the contemporary performance experience been more clearly affirmed than in Arturo Toscanini's combination of scrupulously fanatic attention and supernally dominating musical technique—the fabulous memory, the total grasp of the score, the authoritative understanding of each instrument, and so on. Both during his American career and more or less uninterruptedly since his death, there has been a strenuous debate about Toscanini's achievements, his impressive legacy, his influence on conducting, and his musicianship in general, as well as his shortcomings. It is worth citing as one often quite interesting and provocative monument to the Toscanini debate Joseph Horowitz's 1987 book *Understanding Toscanini*.[15] Horowitz is steeped in the debate, even though his argument that Toscanini's style of taut, literalist objectivism coincided perfectly with the NBC corporate ethos in its ambition to create, Barnum-like, a vast popular audience for classical music is an argument that often either ignores or unjustly diminishes the genuinely electrifying —albeit exaggerated—quality of Toscanini's performances.

On the other hand, for all the generous detail he provides, as well as his admiring yet disapproving accounts of the sometimes unconscious cooperation between Toscanini's narrow aesthetic perspectives and David Sarnoff's corporate ideology, Horowitz does not go as far in severity as Adorno's characterization of Toscanini's Führer-like *Meisterschaft*, based as it is, in Adorno's words, on "iron discipline . . . but precisely iron." In Adorno's view Toscanini's performances, with their predetermined dynamics, their eliminated tensions, and "the protective fixation of the work," obliterate the symphonic work altogether. In Toscanini's performances, control forbids music from going where it might want to go: he is incapable of letting a

---

15. The full title is *Understanding Toscanini: How He Became an American Culture-God and Helped Create a New Audience for Old Music*. I reviewed the book in some detail in *The New York Times Book Review*, March 8, 1987.

phrase "play out," he foregrounds soprano parts (as in Wagner) and "cleans up" complex counterpoint, he refuses to stray from the restricted nineteenth-century repertory that imposes an avoidance either of Baroque or of advanced modern music. Because of this pretended objectivity (*sachlichkeit*) Toscanini for Adorno comes to embody "the triumph of technology and administration over music," even if in performances of Italian opera he produced a sort of exactness (without lingering or sentiment) for which there was no equivalent in the presentation of opera in Germany.[16]

One can actually accept both the Adorno and the Horowitz position—particularly as they discuss Toscanini's complicity in the creation of a basically illiterate mass-market appetite more interested in stereotypes about "the world's greatest conductor conducting the world's greatest music" than in refined and illuminating performances of the kind given by Eugen Jochum, Otto Klemperer, and Wilhelm Furtwängler (all of whom, according to Horowitz, were defeated by Toscanini in America) —that is, one can accept the positions without altogether conceding the point that Toscanini's work clarified what is extreme about the concert occasion itself. This is something I think centrally missing in both their accounts of the Toscanini phenomenon. What stamps the still available 1938 performance by Toscanini of the *Eroica* is the absolute rigor of the logic that he lets unfold in Beethoven's music, and in so doing discloses a process, almost a narrative, that is irreducibly unique, eccentric, contrary to everyday life. So highly wrought is this that it feels like a clear aesthetic alternative to the travails of ordinary human experience.

As Toscanini characteristically takes them, the opening E-flat chords of the *Eroica* announce this process with the distinctive authority of two successive thunderclaps. Thereafter, without a whit of sentimentality or of rubato, the cellos begin the principal theme, passing it to the flutes and horns, until in measure

16. Adorno, "Die Meisterschaft des Maestro," in *Gesammelte Schriften 16* (Frankfurt: Suhrkamp, 1982), p. 66, and *passim*.

41 a gigantic *tutti* recaptures the theme for the full ensemble: all this occurs in a block of time that communicates the rigor and straightforward compression of a wind tunnel, stripped of any sort of palliative adornment or lingering nostalgia. It is not that Toscanini highlights only the melody (as Adorno charged) but that each of the measures of the score is realized with a taut inevitability suggesting the expressivity of pure forward movement that seems to be making only provisional or convenient use of music, rather than communicating the orchestral equivalent of shaped phrasings that derive from the human voice.

What Toscanini seems to me to be doing here is trying to force into prominence, or perhaps enforce, the utterly contrary quality of the performance occasion, its total discontinuity with the ordinary, regular, or normative processes of everyday life. No wonder that Adorno preferred a Furtwängler for whom the performance of, say, the Bruckner or Schubert Ninth symphonies was felt to derive from his private, intuitive interpretation brought out and displayed, as if by the sheerest coincidence, on a public concert platform. In the drier, more unyielding acoustical and expressive contours of a Toscanini performance the concert stage is the public occasion, and *only that;* it stands before us stripped of any vestiges of home, individual subject, family, tradition, or national style. And because it is really very difficult to prove that from a logical point of view Toscanini is wrong, or that concerts under late capitalism are really "music-making" or "communities of interpretation" or shared "subjectivity," and that traditions of performance established in nineteenth-century Berlin and Vienna are being violated, there has been in general an unwillingness to grant that the unrelaxed emotional pressure projected on his audiences by his performances stems immediately from what is extreme in the occasion itself. Out of touch with a reflective composing tradition that was never really his, having lost contact with the vagaries and permissiveness of amateurish musical practice, specialized into the ascetic discipline of a concert repertory based entirely on masterpieces from the past, Toscanini's conducting, I believe, rarified and concentrated the whole business several steps further, and made it for a time *the* dominant musical paradigm. That the paradigm was endorsed and subsidized by a corporate patron is a precise index of business acumen, and of course of the way in which the culture industry operates.

And, I further contend, in its artificiality and restrictive boundaries, the entire mix produces a further clarification, at a notch up from Toscanini, in the career and performances of Glenn Gould. Here I should be perfectly clear about what I do and do *not* mean. I am not saying that Toscanini and Gould are the only performers who are interesting; far from it. I am also not saying that the two of them define all the options for the interpretation and reproduction of Western classical music. I am, however, saying that they elucidate and dramatize the fate of music and music-making as it gets concentrated and constricted into the performance occasion in the period after the one Adorno describes as both heroic and tragic in *Philosophy of Modern Music*. In a society with important ongoing (if perhaps only vestigial) commitments to the central classical canon of the main European tradition, we can say that the concert occasion has superseded the contemporary composer (who, with a few exceptions, has been marginalized by becoming important mainly to other professional composers) or, if the idea of a competition between performer and contemporary composer appears to be too coarse for a cultural phenomenon, we can say that the social configuration in which the concert occasion is the most important factor has provided a wholly separate alternative for the production of music. Whereas a century ago the composer occupied stage center as author and performer, now only the performer (star singer, pianist, violinist, trumpeter, or conductor) remains. There is thus a special importance to be given to a performance that emerges, as Poirier remarks, "out of an accumulation of secretive acts." This, he says, becomes "at last a form that presumes to compete with reality itself for control of the minds exposed to it."

Gould's career as a performing musician begins (almost too

neatly) at just about the time of Toscanini's death in 1957. A recently published biography of Gould by Otto Friedrich provides sufficient detail for us to understand the relentless artificiality and, from the point of view of what is socially and culturally considered to be "normal," the unyieldingly abnormal contours of Gould's life. So strong are they that Gould appears not just unnatural but antinatural, his feelings about his hands, for example, making it impossible and frightening for him as a child even to contemplate playing marbles. In addition, Gould's rather ordinary family (from which he seemed if not estranged then at least disengaged), his calculated solitude and celibacy, his unencumbered and debtless playing style (his only teacher in Toronto appears to have handed on practically none of his ideas to Gould) fostered the illusion of a self-born man, re-creating and even reinventing piano-playing as if from scratch.[17]

Gould died in 1982 at age fifty; yet, as I said earlier, he only played concerts in public for about ten years—between the mid-1950s and the mid-1960s—and after retiring from concert life permanently devoted himself to making records, TV broadcasts, films, and radio programs, most, but not all, featuring him playing the piano. In short, the phenomenally gifted Gould seemed never to have done anything that was not in some way purposefully eccentric. He claimed to avoid the romantic composers (Chopin, Schumann, Liszt, Rachmaninoff) whose work forms the core of the performing pianists' main repertory, and concentrated instead on Bach, or on twentieth century composers like Schoenberg, Krenek, and Hindemith; in addition, he seemed inclined to an odd assortment of other composers (Beethoven, Brahms, Richard Strauss, Sibelius, Bizet, Grieg, and Wagner, for example) whose work he sometimes approached as no one else did, often playing compositions by them that no other pianist played. On occasion he played works he did not

17. Otto Friedrich, *Glenn Gould: A Life and Variations* (New York: Random House, 1989); see pp. 15–16 for the story about Gould's not playing marbles, his unwillingness to catch a tennis ball, etc.

like by composers he seemed to disdain: his nearly integral recording of the Mozart piano sonatas is a case in point, and even though other musicians have also performed works they did not care for, no one except Gould advertised the fact and played accordingly.

Gould's astounding virtuosity and rhythmic grace produced a sound ideally suited to making complex music sound clearer and more intelligently understood and organized than the sound produced by other pianists. His first recording, Bach's *Goldberg Variations*, was made when he was barely out of his teens, but the work's extraordinary contrapuntal logic, its dazzlingly beautiful and yet rigorous structures, its brilliant keyboard configurations were rendered by the young pianist with a pianistic flair that was unprecedented. And that of course is the principal point to be made about Gould's sound, his style, and his entire deportment: his complete separation from the world of other pianists, of other people, of other prerogatives. His career seemed to be constructed like a self-conscious counternarrative to the careers of all other musicians. Once the initial constraints were understood and accepted by Gould the rest of what he did can be read retrospectively to have followed consequentially.

These constraints—together with the discipline they impose constituting what I have been calling "performance as an extreme occasion"—were those provided by the frame of the performance itself and, within that, by the illusion of the performer's inaccessibility to the routine demands not just of other performing styles but also of human life as lived by other human beings. Friedrich's book makes that point with almost devastating force. Gould neither ate, slept, nor behaved socially like anyone else. He kept himself alive with drugs, his musical and intellectual habits were ringed with insomnia and endless quasi-clinical self-observation, and in every way imaginable he allowed himself to be absorbed into a sort of airless but pure performance enclave that in turn paradoxically kept reminding one of the very concert platform he had deserted.

Occasionally what Gould did seemed as if he was stepping past the platform into a strange world beyond it.

Gould's direct appropriation of Bach from the very outset of his career can be seen retrospectively to have been a brilliantly right, that is strategically created, beginning. Listen to the opening theme of the *Goldberg* Variations as he recorded the work in 1955: the listener will be struck by the unprotected directness of the proleptic announcement the theme makes (as if the gigantic work is somehow secreted within the theme in fragile outline), not just of the vastly proliferating variations that Bach elaborated out of it, but also of Gould's fantastically brilliant performing style, its heady brashness even in quiet moments, its unidiomatic heightening of the piano's percussive traits, its fearless negotiation of the most elaborate patterns and configurations. Gould used the *Goldberg* as a way of immediately setting himself apart from other debut recitalists (whose choice of repertory was always more predictable than his), as if instead of continuing the romantic tradition that sustained virtuoso performers, Gould was starting *his* pedigree earlier than theirs and then vaulting past them into the present.

Thereafter Gould recorded the Partitas, both books of the *Well-Tempered Clavier*, the Toccatas, the English and French suites, the inventions and short preludes and fugues, plus a major section of the *Art of Fugue;* some concerted pieces (concerti and violin and gamba sonatas) were also performed and recorded. What stands out in all this is not so much a uniform style but a clear and immediately impressive continuity of attack and rhetorical address that, during the decades he performed in public, was italicized and highlighted by a massive catalogue of mannerisms—humming, conducting, low chair, slouch, etc. Even a short series of extracts from his recordings reveals the clarity of voices, the rhythmic inventiveness, and the effortless tonal and digital logic that permits an unbroken continuity of identity and performing signature to emerge.

I suggest, for instance, a handful of preludes and fugues from the *Well-Tempered Clavier*, in which what in effect is a

solemn, didactic exercise is refurbished by Gould, is trans-
formed into a set of mood pieces, strictly delivered in correctly
realized contrapuntal style, but always phrased, shaped, and
rendered into a completely integrated characterization. His recording of the Toccatas, like that of the French Suites, gives the
dance-inspired movements an astonishing vividness that separates them entirely from their social origins, and transfigures
them into abstract typifications of particular rhythms and syn-
copations. Using the same technique Gould turned to a set of
what are known as "little" preludes, a recording of one of
which (BWV 933 in C major) delivers a fascinating study of
interweaving patterns—turns with arpeggiated chords, running passages with highlighted themes—kept bright and bustling by the acutely stressed operation of Gould's rhythmical
vitality.

None of the remarkable things that Gould does, however,
would have been possible without a truly rare digital mecha-
nism that easily rivals those of "legendary" technicians like
Vladimir Horowitz, Jorge Bolet, Arturo Benedetti Michelangeli,
and one or two others. Gould always seemed to achieve a
seamless unity among his fingers, the piano, and the music he
was playing, one working by extension *into* the other, the three
becoming indistinguishable from start to finish. It was as if
Gould's virtuosity finally derived its fluency from the piece and
not from a residue of technical athleticism built up indepen-
dently over the years. Pollini has some of the same quality as
Gould in this respect, but it is the wonderfully intelligent exercise of his fingers in polyphonic music that separates Gould
from every other pianist. Only a great Bach organist communicates in something like the same way, except that as a concert
pianist Gould had an awareness of the essentially theatrical
frame that calls attention to what keeps him on the distinct side
of the divide between audience and performer.

But two more things about Gould distinguished him from
other pianists. I have already mentioned the first. In 1964 he
stopped playing concerts and, as I said, completely left public

"live" performing in order to devote himself to recording, writing, and composing. Although his career on concert stages had been very successful, he said he quit "live" performances because, he now argued, they distorted the music theatrically, on the one hand, and on the other hand, concert-giving did not allow him the necessary "take-twoness" of the recording studio, the opportunity to replay sections of music requiring further elaboration and polish.

The second of Gould's fateful attributes was his exceptional —if not prodigal—verbal gift, to which he gave increasingly wider play after he was no longer performing concerts (he began by giving lectures during the 1960s). Unlike many performing musicians, he seemed to have not only ideas and a mind but the ability to apply them to music both as performer and as critic. His performances, in short, approximated to an argument, and his discursive arguments were often borne out by his pianistic feats. This was never more evident (as we shall see presently) than in the remarkable series of films made about Gould by various British, Canadian, French, and German directors, films that allowed Gould to speak, perform, illustrate his ideas with scintillating wit, and to considerable effect, in settings that were a hybrid of living-room, practice studio, and lecture hall. He was thus musician, teacher, "personality," and performer all at once.

To take from Gould one or another of these various roles is to end up with an actually *more* improbable, less interesting phenomenon. As a writer Gould, I think, requires the piano and the immediacy of his lively presence to make what he says work. The published material, collected in a one-volume potpourri of essays, articles, and record liners, is often overwritten and underargued.[18] There are garrulous displays of wit and parody that are, to my taste, both forced and insufferably tedious. Gould was neither intellectually disciplined nor a fully cultivated man, and his learning, for all the exuberance with

18. *The Glenn Gould Reader*, ed. Tim Page (New York: Alfred A. Knopf, 1984).

which he deployed it, often reveals the trying awkwardness of the naive village philosopher. The paradox is that his writings are nevertheless essential as the verbal counterpoint he provided for himself as a performer. Thus quite deliberately Gould extended the limited theatrical space provided by performance as an extreme occasion to one whose scope includes speech, time as duration, an interlude from daily life that is not controlled by mere consecutiveness. Thus for Gould performance was an inclusive phenomenon but it was still kept within the bounds and the inaccessibility imposed by his studied eccentricity. In addition, his performances were unmistakably affiliated with aspects of the contemporary technological and cultural environment, especially his longtime relationships with CBS records and the Canadian Broadcasting Corporation.

There is something Jamesian about the last part of Gould's career: he can be interpreted like one of the symbolic figures appearing in Henry James's parables of the 1880s that were meditations on both the problems of the craft of writing and the personality of the artist. One can imagine James fashioning a story about an artist called Glenn Gould who after ten years of concerts at the mercy of ticket-holders, schedules, and impresarios decides to become the author of his own scripts and so forces upon the whole process of performance—which is, after all, what *he* has been condemned to in the age of specialization—his own individualistic transformation: he invites friends home to perform for them. Gould's audience nonetheless continued to hear in the records that he was to make during his post concert-giving period the same recognizable stylistic signature, although now—if we take his record of Wagner transcriptions as an instance of the new transformation—the playing has expanded from Bach into a late twentieth-century transcription of late nineteenth-century Wagnerian counterpoint and melody, conveyed in the modern idiom already pioneered by Gould for the contemporary piano.

The most typically Gouldian extracts are the *Meistersinger* prelude and his considerably edited version of the *Siegfried*

*Idyll*. The orchestral piece that begins Wagner's only comic opera is seen by Gould as no conductor or orchestra has ever played it: it becomes a compendium of eighteenth-century contrapuntal writing displayed for an audience with a sort of anatomical glee by Gould, who plays the piece with such neat virtuosity as to make you forget that human hands are involved. Near the end, as Wagner's orchestral writing becomes too thick and the number of simultaneous themes too great even for Gould, the pianist resorts (he tells us in a liner note) to overdubbing, superimposing his recording of one part of the dense score on his recording of another part. This is as if by doubling the electronic prerogatives of the performing occasion Gould had exponentially also increased the rarity and power of the performer's hold on the duration of a concert favorite. In his transcription of the *Siegfried Idyll* Gould tampers with Wagner's notes so as somewhat to reduce the similarity between piano transcription and orchestra original in order to elevate the special character of a twentieth-century pianistic reproduction. In both instances, however, Gould's ideas of Wagner are supplementally reinforced by his prose notes for the record jacket.

As Gould seems to have suspected, his choice of Wagner itself would be most fully commented on not just by playing his ideas, so to speak, but also by his "additional" prose. Note that Gould's ideas are worth looking into not so much only because they are of inherent validity (they have, for instance a fascinating resonance in the Canadian context as shown by B. W. Powe in *The Solitary Outlaw*)[19] but because they also show us Gould grappling publicly with his predicament as a performing pianist who discursively notes everything that he can comment on as pianist and as critic along the way. As such, then, Gould's observations furnish the most intense example of the performance occasion being forcibly pulled out of the tired routine and unthinking consensus that ordinarily support the

19. B. W. Powe, *The Solitary Outlaw: Trudeau, Lewis, Gould, Canetti, McLuhan* (Toronto: Lester and Orpen Dennys, 1987).

concert performance as a relatively lifeless social form. But what I am also saying is that Gould's restless forays into writing, radio, television, and film enhanced, enlivened, and illuminated his playing itself, giving it a self-conscious aesthetic and cultural presence whose aim, while not always clear, was to enable performance to engage or to affiliate with the world itself, without compromising the essentially reinterpretive, reproductive quality of the process. This, I think, is the Adornian measure of Gould's achievement, and also its limitations, which are those of a late capitalism that has condemned classical music to an impoverished marginality and anti-intellectualism sheltered underneath the umbrella of "autonomy." Yet like Toscanini before him, Gould sets the standard by which in an art without an easily graspable ideological or social value (perhaps an aspect of what Poirier calls its moral neutrality and innocence) it could itself be interpreted.

From his writing it seems quite clear that Gould saw nothing at all exceptional about playing the piano well. What he wanted was an escape from everything that determined or conditioned his reality as a human being. Consider, for example, that his favorite state was "ecstasy," his favorite music was music ideally not written for specific instruments and hence "essentially incorporeal," and his highest words of praise were *repose, detachment, isolation.* To this, Friedrich's biography contributes the notion of *control,* which is the motif of much of Gould's life. Moreover, Gould seems to have believed that art was "mysterious," but that it allowed "the gradual, life-long construction of a state of wonder and serenity" that, when conveyed through radio and recordings, shapes "the elements of aesthetic narcissism" and responds "to the challenge that each man contemplatively creates his own divinity."[20]

This is not complete metaphysical nonsense, at least not if it is read as a comment on Gould's peculiar situation. He seems to have been finally discontent both with the nonverbal, non-

<hr>

20. *The Glenn Gould Reader,* pp. 331–57. See also Payzant, note 22, below.

discursive nature of music—its silence about itself—and with the actual physical achievement of being a performing pianist. In the amusing interviews he did with Jonathan Cott in 1974, first published in *Rolling Stone* and now done up as a little book adorned with handsome photographs,[21] Gould speaks with laughable exaggeration of being able to teach anyone the skills of pianism in half an hour. Elsewhere he says he hardly practiced or bothered with playing the piano for its own sake. He was more interested in those aspects of music and of his own talents that spilled over from musical expression into language, in how the daily reminders of his indebtedness both to composer and to audience might be transmuted into the utopia of an infinitely changeable and extendable world where time or history did not occur, and because of which all expression was transparent, logical, and not hampered by flesh-and-blood performers or people at all.

Considered as the record of Gould's lifelong struggle to be *more* than just a performing pianist, his prose is thus eminently worth consideration. Whether Gould's writing is a sign that he regarded his career as a luxury item to be transcended, or whether his verbal energies concealed the deeper personal crisis of someone with nowhere really to go, as afraid of maturity as of commitment to the processes of life in human society, I cannot say. But beneath the tinkle of his often cheerful words there lurks something far less assured and satisfied than Gould's tone explicitly permits: of that one can be certain.

Perhaps the most interesting thing about Gould's writing is how it seems like an attempt to extend his ideas about musical performance into other realms. And clearly his writings remind one of Gould's music, not because they refer specifically to or summarize how he plays, but in the way they touch one with their restless energy and their remorseless articulation of meanings, neither stable nor fully attainable. There is much the same play of counterpoint here between words and performance that

21. Jonathan Cott, *Conversations with Glenn Gould* (New York: Little, Brown, 1984).

one also hears in Gould's recordings of Bach fugues. Their sheer vitality makes such experiences rare and precious as a result.

Another dimension is added by Gould's films, the most interesting and riveting of which show Gould performing pieces either contrapuntal (fugues and canons, mainly) or variational in nature. One hour-long program is devoted to fugue, and it comprises selections from Bach's *Well-Tempered Clavier,* the last movement of Beethoven's opus 110 sonata, and a stunningly fluent and demonic rendition of the last fugal movement of Hindemith's Third Sonata, a fine piece hardly ever played in concert today for reasons that have to do with the intellectual cowardice and low aesthetic standards of a majority of today's musicians, which Gould's career as a whole so strenuously impugns.

The variations program climaxes with performances of Webern's *Variations* and Beethoven's E major Sonata, opus 109. Gould links the two by a brilliant highlighting of the structural finesse and expressive detail that is so similar in both works. This is a considerable achievement since the pieces are written out of tonal idioms with diametrically opposed consequences, one (Beethoven's) exfoliative and elaborate, the other (Webern's) concentrated and crabbed. In addition, Gould delivers a severely restrained performance of a Sweelinck Organ Fantasy on the same program. I recall hearing it during a Gould recital in 1959 or 1960, struck at the time (and again in watching the film) by how Gould could apparently disappear as a performer into the work's long complications, thereby providing an instance of the *ecstasy* he characterized as the state of standing outside time and within an integral artistic structure.

Yet by far the most moving and affecting of all of Gould's films is Bruno Monsaingeon's 1981 rendition of Gould as he first speaks about, then plays through, the *Goldberg* Variations. Gould in this film is no longer the lean and youthfully eager intellectual who has the caustic wit to say (as he does in an earlier film) of Beethoven that he was always going to meet his

destiny at the next modulation. He has now become a potbel-
lied, bald, and somewhat mournful middle-aged aesthete whose
jowly face and slightly decadent lips suggest secret vices and
too many rich meals. Even his fingers, which have retained
their fabulously efficient elegance and economy, are now evidently older, and more worldly. Indeed, Gould's performance
of these thirty extraordinary pieces has acquired layers of so-
phistication and cleverness in added ornaments, in oddly varied and usually slower tempi, in surprising repetitions, in more
sharply inflected lines (for example, the heavily strummed bass
line in Variation One, or the underlinings of the theme in
Bach's unison canon in the Third Variation, etc.).

This is one of the very few films I have seen of Gould that is
in color and quite obviously the work of a film-maker, not
simply of a TV cameraman. Its autumnal hues are made more
startling by the realization that this was to be Gould's very last
performance of, fittingly enough, the work that first brought
him widespread attention: it is impossible not to imagine the
film as an act of closure. I was told by Professor Geoffrey
Payzant of the University of Toronto (a philosopher whose
excellent book on Gould is the only work on the pianist even to
begin to do him some justice)[22] that Monsaingeon had a cache
of 52 hour-long films of Gould performances that he was trying
unsuccessfully to sell to various TV companies in Europe and
the United States. But, I think, Monsaingeon was right so
singlemindedly to want to film Gould at work: the man was
quite literally a full-scale cultural enterprise, endlessly at work
on performance.

But the most interesting thing about Gould is, as Monsaingeon saw, that he constantly oversteps boundaries and bursts
confining restraints, thereby, sometimes poignantly sometimes
comically, *confirming* the performance space itself. In 1987 Monsaingeon himself published a book about Gould in France whose
last section is a "video montage" of Gould being interviewed

22. Geoffrey Payzant, *Glenn Gould, Music and Mind* (1978; Toronto: Key Porter
Books, 1984).

by five critics *after his death:*[23] Clearly Monsaingeon saw the man as someone for whom ordinary mortality was no limit at all. Gould certainly cultivated this notion in his audience. Not only was it clear that Gould could, and in fact did (with a few puzzling omissions, noted by Friedrich), command the entire range of Western music from the Renaissance until the present —there are instances in some of the films of Gould talking away about a series of musical examples and then turning to the piano, illustrating them from memory—he also could do with it what he liked, improvise, transpose, parody, reproduce, etc.

Most good musicians do in fact have at their fingertips, or lips, or hearts, much more music than they perform in public. Memory is part of the gift every performer carries within, so to speak. Yet we see performances only on the stage, *in* a program confined by the performance occasion itself. Thus Gould went to very great lengths after he left the concert stage in 1964 to communicate his diverse talents to an audience as he spilled out his knowledge, his articulate analyses, his prodigious technical facility into other forms and styles well beyond the two-hour concert experience. Everything that Gould did was in a continuum with the original place and time that he had been afforded as a performer, the concert platform. And whenever he seemed to have settled into a niche, say, as a Bach pianist, he would up and record Wagner transcriptions, or the Grieg sonata, repertory that could not have been more unexpected, or he would become a writer, or a television personality.

Most important in all this, however, was Gould's talent for doing one thing brilliantly (playing the piano well, for example) and suggesting that he was doing something else too. Hence his predilection for contrapuntal or variational forms or, on a slightly different level, his habit of playing the piano *and* conducting *and* singing, or his way of being able to quote both musically and intellectually more or less any thing at any time.

23. *Glenn Gould: Non, je ne suis pas de tout un excentrique,* montage et presentation de Bruno Monsaingeon (Paris: Fayard, 1986).

In a sense then Gould was gradually moving toward a kind of nontheatrical and anti-aesthetic *Gesamtkunstwerk*, a description that sounds antiformal and contradictory at the same time. I am not sure how aware he was of this, and how conscious he was of Rimbaud's *deracinement du sens*, but it strikes me as apt since the idea seems to me to approach the unsettling and yet attractively intelligent qualities in Gould's unusual enterprise, which was at once to make the performance more—because packed, bustling, overflowing—of an occasion, and more extreme, more odd, more unlike the lived reality of humankind, and still more unlike other concerts. By its radical force Gould's career in fine has supplied us with a largely but not completely new concept of what performance is all about, which like most things in musical elaboration—because it is still ideologically and commercially linked to the past and to present society—is neither a total disruption nor a total transformation of customary practice.

The distensions and peculiarities in what Gould did may in time come to seem totally innocuous, tamed or incorporated by the ongoing culture business, of which classical musical performance is only one component. An index of this diminishment to Gould's real activity is that he is known today almost exclusively either as a curiosity or as a very gifted pianist, just as Toscanini is known entirely as a great conductor about whose interpretations one may have opinions, but the social and aesthetic meanings of whose career are now generally screened from attention or study. The critical discourse of ongoing musical performance allows itself to report on concert life only in the manner of a scoresheet. But when we look from the rigid (and rigidly enforced) habits of concert life and journalism to the more extravagant excursions of performance art or rock music, only then can we assess the resourcefulness and imagination at work in performers like Toscanini or Gould who first accepted, then elaborated the logic of what contemporary classical music offered them, and did so with at least some measure of self-consciousness and spirit.

# On the Transgressive
# Elements in Music

In thinking about or experiencing any of the arts we are inevitably led to a discussion about what is intrinsic and what extrinsic to a particular work. In recent cultural or literary criticism a greatly debated matter concerns the way in which so-called canons, or lists of great works, are constituted. Is the Western canon of essential books from Homer to Dostoievsky, for example, something that reflects the interests of a class, a coterie, or a nationalist group, or is it intrinsically what is best, inherently authentic, irreducibly great in Western literature? This sort of question in turn gives rise to others of the kind that especially attach to issues of morality and judgment. Having for some years been very concerned with these debates, I'd like to reflect on them now in a context that includes the specifically musical matters I want to discuss here.

In the recent controversy surrounding the personality, pedagogy, and theories of the late Paul de Man we can distinguish what separates most (but not all) of the participants into two opposed camps. One thesis and its supporters then is that having been a columnist for *Le Soir* during the Nazi occupation of Belgium—*Le Soir* being an openly collaborationist newspaper—de Man acted with the Occupation, his anti-Semitic articles constituting the main proof of villainy; this villainy is in turn adduced to condemn not only his later silence about some of his wartime activities but also his theories of the period during which he became a distinguished American academic. While usually accepting the fact of de Man's collaboration, the opposed camp absolves the older man who had become a major American theorist from most of the early villainy, suggesting instead—and here I simplify egregiously—that as the work of a brilliant critic, de Man's writing after World War II rises above its earlier biographical and political encumbrances.

Many other things are involved here: the outrage of already suspicious opponents of theory, deconstruction, de Man himself; the loyalty of his friends and students, several of whom have not completely dodged the difficulty of the challenge, yet all of whom have consistently testified to the extraordinary qualities of the man they knew as mind and person; the overdeveloped taste for gossip and scandal; the moralistic cant of preaching journalists, pundits, conservative professors; the earnest zeal of historians, amateur as well as professional, for whom the de Man case is an occasion for new research and suggestive conclusions; the miasmic effusions of various self-appointed sages. One could go on giving reasons for the interest of the de Man case and the amount of time spent debating it, but buried beneath the whole deeply compelling controversy is the question of whether moral and political affiliation or guilt in the world of everyday life can have a serious bearing upon the quality and interpretation of works of mind, works that are principally aesthetic and intellectual in which matters of fact are only tangentially at issue.

Back of that question, of course, is the problem of authorship. When T. S. Eliot made the distinction between the poet as poet, and the person who has a personality, suffers, and has a psychology, he did little to settle the distinction once and for all: he simply articulated it with eye-catching skill as a problem. For are we to conclude that brilliant writers who were also the authors of scurrilous racist tracts—Céline, Carlyle, Pound, the list is extendable—are to be looked at in exactly the same way as are the authors of great poetry, ideas, fiction, philosophical analysis who lived relatively blameless lives? Does the author of discreditable work, by virtue of belonging to a common world of discourse or *Zeitgeist*, attach to or in some other way infect by association the altogether creditable work of the intellectually and aesthetically preferable author? Conversely most of us will allow that if an artist has a life of distinction and "human interest" on aesthetic and (presumably) moral grounds, knowledge of that life can stimulate a greater appreciation of his or her works; this has certainly been the case with Dr. Johnson, Conrad, George Eliot, T. E. Lawrence, Malraux.

I have barely begun to list all the permutations and possible articulations of what might be regarded as E. M. Forster's admonishment "to connect" things with each other, and I shall not even try to be exhaustive. What I want to assert is the intuitive conviction I have—and I think most of us have—that what we are dealing with in most of the instances I have listed is not the separation between art or theory and life but rather the already powerful, commonsensical, and experiential connection between them. There are reasons for, and there is an interest in, separating them but, I maintain, these two spheres of human effort exist together, they live together, they *are* together. In the de Man case the reason for separating his earlier from his later work (or for connecting them to each other) is to assess responsibility and to decide about consequences of the sort that are contained in such questions as: if he had been a collaborator with the Nazis, how then could he have written excellent work later; or, another formulation, is his later work the result, the direct result (either because he tried to hide or abjure it), of his condemnable earlier ideas, and therefore just as condemnable; or, yet another version, what are the consequences for deconstructive theory or de Manian ideas generally if one can prove that their author was (and perhaps remained) a crypto-Nazi? Is there any way of reading and enjoying with profit works like *Allegories of Reading* and *Blindness and Insight,* given that the whole controversy has polarized, debilitated, and, alas, reduced the level of discourse to a rhetoric either of pure defensiveness or of blame, neither of which is of much assistance once we get past the relatively elementary point of diametrically opposed asseveration and resolute denial?

Let me add something here that may appear to be so irrelevant and so idiosyncratic as to be trivial, but which I think at least needs saying. In the most offensive of his *Le Soir* articles (March 4, 1941) de Man says that "one thus sees that a solution of the Jewish problem which would aim at the creation of a Jewish colony isolated from Europe, would not entail deplorable consequences for the literary life of the West." [1] None of the commentators I have read glosses one especially sinister resonance in the phrase "the creation of a Jewish colony isolated from Europe." You do not have to be a Palestinian to know that in 1941 there already was a Jewish colony outside Europe, already the locale of conflict between native Palestinians and incoming Zionist settlers, already the topic of an enormous amount of international jurisprudential, rhetorical, political, religious, and other controversy. For me, to read de Man's remark has been to wait in vain for someone who would note how in an anti-Semitic, brazenly collaborationist, and pro-Nazi paper an author seemed to be in fact not just recommending the Zionist project already underway (with perhaps an allusion also to the short-lived Nazi plan to settle Jews in Madagascar), [2] already entailing the onset of Palestinian dispossession, but to be doing so casually, almost backhandedly, as if the real subject was the health of Europe, not the disaster to be visited upon at least three generations of Palestinians. What has made de Man's little comment no less awful to contemplate has been the star-

1. Paul de Man, *Wartime Journalism, 1939–1943,* ed. Werner Hamacker, Neil Hertz, and Thomas Keenan (Lincoln: University of Nebraska Press, 1988), p. 45.
2. See Michael R. Marrus and Robert O. Paxton, *Vichy France and the Jews* (New York: Schocken Books, 1981), pp. 59–61, 112–13.

tling juxtaposition in it of a direct link between the wish to be rid of the Jews for the cultural health of Europe and the question of Palestine.

But having begun to unravel the knot we should proceed further and say that de Man's passing reference to Zionism is a dramatic confirmation of the links between right-wing and even fascist European thought and Zionism itself, a link quickly overlooked during the immediate postwar period, when the drive to establish a Jewish state in Palestine accelerated and in fact became, in the Western context, a progressive idea. There is some irony to be remarked that when in the early 1980s the American scholar Lenni Brenner published a book entitled *Zionism in the Age of the Dictators*[3] and showed a whole series of active connections between right-wing Zionism—whose most famous living representative is Yitzhak Shamir—and officials of the Third Reich, including Adolf Eichmann, the evidence was not even discussed in the popular or public sphere; by "evidence" I mean letters exchanged, details of person-to-person contacts, and so on. With even greater and perhaps more bitter irony, given the recent twist and turns of the Salman Rushdie affair, with British and American writers falling all over each other in the admirably sanctioned cause of defending Rushdie's right to speak and publish against Ayatollah Khomeini's threats, it was once again forgotten that barely two years before, in January 1987, a British playwright, Jim Allen, had his play *Perdition* banned and cleared off the boards of London's Royal Court Theater because in the play he told the story of wartime collaboration in Europe between Zionist and Nazi officials, a story also told in Edwin Black's *The Transfer Agreement*.[4] Few of the intellectuals who now correctly defended

3. Lenni Brenner, *Zionism in the Age of the Dictators: A Reappraisal* (Westport: Lawrence Hill, 1983).

4. Jim Allen, *Perdition: A Play in Two Acts* (London: Ithaca Press, 1987). This printed version of the play also includes a full selection of newspaper articles, commentary, and analysis provoked by the play. See also Edwin Black's *The Transfer Agreement: The Untold Story of the Secret Pact Between the Third Reich and Jewish Palestine* (New York: Macmillan, 1984).

Rushdie had previously come to Allen's side, and the play disappeared from public knowledge; I was told by a British friend in 1988 that there had been an attempt to videotape one performance of the play assembled exclusively for the occasion, but that too was prevented from happening. Thus so dense, intertwined, and extended a mass is the real web of circumstances given rise to by any reflection on the de Man case, so surprising its twists and turns, so unexpected its ramifications, so much does it depend on which person with what history writes about it, that it is all we can do to inventory them accurately. So we are still at a moment close enough to the events of de Man's death and the rediscovery of his wartime writings to be dealing with what is far from a separation between external and internal aspects of his theories but is in reality a rush of convergences that, depending on the interpreter, will highlight some and obscure others.

The letters and words of literary texts are of course denotative; they share a common, and overlapping, discursivity with spoken language in ways that, with the exception of a rudimentary onomatopoeic mimicry, are very different from the relationship between musical notes and words. Music is not denotative and does not share a common discursivity with language. Nevertheless, a similar, albeit much more grandiose and often coarser set of convergences emerges in any discussion of Wagner and, to a lesser degree, of Richard Strauss. Both are performed with considerable frequency all over Europe and the United States, but, with the exception of a single recent performance in Israel by Zubin Mehta and the Israel Philharmonic, Wagner is not performed, is in fact proscribed from performance, in Israel. Strauss, however, is performed although his reputation in Israel is (to use an awful euphemism) controversial. The reasons given for Wagner's prohibition are that he was an openly proclaimed anti-Semite and that both his ideological and aesthetic accounts of his own music as an emanation from German and Western European art depend to an appreciable degree upon his attempts to exclude, to excoriate, and, it is suggested, to exterminate what he calls the Jewish character. These repulsive ideas of his are so well known as to constitute today, almost 150 years after the fact, an *idée reçue*. Yet because Bayreuth and members of the Wagner family (especially Winifred) were especially close to Hitler and Hitler's thought, there remains an unarguably close association in many minds between Wagner's music-dramas and the whole ghastly history of the Nazi onslaught upon humanity generally, the Jews in particular. The contamination is so great that any attempt to excuse Wagner for the fact that he died well before Hitler's ascendancy appears ridiculously, not to say mendaciously, ineffective.

Adorno was right to have argued that Wagner's hatred of Jews—which appears with some clarity in his portraits of Beckmesser, Mime, and Alberich—is irreducible, and he is shrewd further to suggest that this anti-Semitism is what Walter Benjamin defined as disgust, "the fear of being thought to be the same as that which is found disgusting." [5] Yet the coincidences between Wagner and Nazism—Adorno later calls Wagner the willing prophet of imperialism and terrorism—are too close to pass by. There is, to pick only a couple of irresistibly obvious examples, the use of words that echo monstrously out of an opera, in one case *Das Rheingold*, where Alberich rules over Niebelheim with his gold ring, and, in employing the Tarnhelm to dominate his frightened brother, says: *Nacht und Nebel,/ Niemand gleich*, the very words of the infamous Nazi order for the death camps. Or there is the considerably less fraught case of Hans Sachs in the final concerted scene of *Die Meistersinger* addressing the crowds on the salutary virtues of "holy German art," and the threat to it from alien, unwelcome influences.

The sinister chromaticism of the Tarnhelm motif can quite easily be interpreted as the evil and unhealthy preparation for the Nazi onset half a century later; and in Alberich's willing acceptance of lovelessness and damnation his unremitting de-

5. Theodor Adorno, *In Search of Wagner*, trans. Rodney Livingstone (London: New Left Books, 1981), p. 24.

sire for world conquest adumbrates the appalling designs of
the 1000–year Reich. Sachs's altogether less pathological-seem-
ing sentiments at the very end of *Die Meistersinger* nevertheless
prefigure certain aspects of twentieth century German xeno-
phobia. To the assembled population of Nuremberg he preaches
a doctrine of German art that, were it to be threatened by
foreign influences or conquest, might lose its most beneficial
aspects. Therefore he preaches vigilance and a disquietingly
authoritarian doctrine of unquestioning compliance with the
powers-that-be ("ehrt eure deutschen Meister!"). That Alberich's music is angular and chromatic, Sachs's (except for his
brief mention of outside threats) diatonically solid, is part of
Wagner's awareness of how easily music can adapt itself to
worldly situations, and this is surely the very core of Wagner's
supreme gift for program and narrative music.

It does not lessen but actually compounds the problems that
the musical styles of these two cases derive from and lead to
music whose aesthetic status is unimpeachable. Alberich delivers his sinister lines in a harmonically advanced idiom whose
subsequent development will account for such towering figures
as Richard Strauss, Bruckner, Mahler, Debussy, and of course
Schoenberg, the last a revolutionary in music and later in life a
deeply conservative proto-monarchist Jew, one of whose eth-
nic/nationalist works (aside from *Moses und Aron*) was a Zionist
drama, *Der biblische Weg*, based on Theodor Herzl, or rather on
his enterprise as reinterpreted by Schoenberg.[6] On the other
hand, Sachs's address is immediately obvious as belonging to,
and prepared for by, the long tradition of German choral music, whose monuments are Bach and Handel. There is therefore
deliberation in the continuity affirmed between Wagner and his
illustrious predecessors, especially in his insistence upon the
affinity between his choral polyphony and the essentially eccle-
siastical context of the earlier masters. Thus the first scene of

6. There is an illuminating discussion of this in Herbert Lindenberger, "Arnold
Schoenberg's *Der biblische Weg* and *Moses und Aron*: On the Transactions of Aesthetics and Politics," *Modern Judaism* 9 (1989): 55–70.

EXAMPLE 3. Wagner's *Die Meistersinger*, opening chorus of Act I

*Die Meistersinger* is set in a church in which the chorale sung by
the people of Nuremberg bears a strong formal and doctrinal
resemblance to the triumphant choral anthem at the end of the
opera, a few minutes before Sachs sings his valedictory salute
to German art (Example 3). The great final C-major cadences of
the Prelude go directly to the C-major tonic of the chorale
(which is further consolidated by the organ Wagner's scoring
explicitly requires) whose first line, "Da zu dir der Heiland
kam" (as our Savior came to thee), sanctifies Nuremberg and
its people. The final chorale ("Wach' auf") echoes one of the
most famous of German Lutheran chorales, although Wagner's
melody is assertively carried forward as a motivic transformation of his *Meistersinger* theme (Example 4).

Clearly Wagner wanted not only to dragoon the positive
valences of Christianity and its musical idiom into his own

EXAMPLE 4. *Die Meistersinger*, final chorale

EXAMPLE 5. Extract from Beckmesser's prize song, Act III of *Die Meistersinger*

service but also to exclude, and thereafter stamp as non-German and foreign, all the sickly, overlearned, ridiculously hypocritical, and consequently unmusical traits realized by Beckmesser, whose prize song is an unintentional neurotic parody not only of Walther's prize song but also of Sachs's Act II vulgar cobbling ditty about Eve's aching feet after she leaves Paradise (Example 5).

There is a relentless mirror effect in all this (and of course in the whole system of *leitmotiven*) designed to reinforce Wagner's musical and dramatic point, which, as Thomas Mann's *Doctor Faustus* was so powerfully to grasp, could be seen as directly symbolic of totalitarianism. Adorno speaks of this aspect of Wagner in the mid-1930s, but his account stresses its deleterious aesthetic effects on the music: "What specifically characterized Wagnerian expression," he writes, "is its intentionality: the *leitmotiv* is a sign that transmits a particle of congealed meaning." [7] The result, Adorno claims, is a style hobbled by innumerable limitations, although the paradoxical fully-intended effect of the music is of a never-ending melody. In *Faustus* Mann seizes upon the dizzyingly productive aspects of this and similar *aperçus,* and elevates them to the principle of National Socialism. Adrian Leverkühn's pact with the devil is therefore a peculiarly apt fable for a musician whose technical interests replicate the parallelism possible between the least denotative and most formal of the arts, music, and life conceived in a Nietzschean mode amorally, beyond good and evil.

We need very briefly to recall some of these parallelisms here: Adrian's fascination with inanimate objects that imitate the behavior of real life; his interest in the "elemental," which leads him to Beethoven, theology, the C-major triad; the aspiration of art to become knowledge; dissonance as polyphony, and therefore as something rich and full of possibility; the correspondence between music and theology; and later, music as the intermediary in the marriage between mathematics and theology. When Adrian encounters the devil he is offered the possibility in music of going beyond the whole canon of classical music—the devil calls it "elaboration"—which in the late romantic period has become unacceptable cliché, totally socialized, and trivial even if autonomous. Originality cannot be derived from health because the canon form, which in its regulated permutations is Mann's symbol of a historical time ruled over by God, has exhausted all the possible combinations of notes. Therefore parody and critique propose themselves as the

7. Adorno, *In Search of Wagner*, pp. 44–45.

only true novelty in so overripe and exhausted a period, and their equivalents in the life of the truly gifted individual are disease and the barbarism of the elemental, which exist outside time and culture, and beyond the scope of anything elaborated in ordinary duration.

The supernaturally granted aptitude therefore to defy time and humanity will confer a new demonic power upon Adrian because the gift offers a sudden access of transcendence. The principle is stated by the devil:

> an untruth of a kind that enhances power holds its own against any ineffectively virtuous truth. And I mean too that creative, genius-giving disease, disease that rides on high horse over all hindrances, and springs with drunken daring from peak to peak, is a thousand times dearer to life than plodding healthiness. . . . [Therefore the devil forecasts admirable success for Adrian.] You will lead the way, you will strike up the march of the future, the lads will swear by your name, who thanks to your madness will no longer need to be mad. On your madness they will feed in health, and in them you will become healthy. . . . Not only will you break through the paralysing difficulties of the time—you will break through time itself, by which I mean the cultural epoch and its cult, and dare to be barbaric, twice barbaric indeed, because of coming after the humane, after all possible root-treatment and bourgeois raffinement.[8]

To this promise Mann assimilates the horrific fate of modern Germany, perhaps even of Western civilization itself. Music's fundamental muteness allows Mann, as it allows Leverkühn and Adorno—whose musicological philosophy of the degeneration inscribed in the critique and the dehumanized alienation of Beethoven's late or third period style (particularly as Beethoven moves from the developmental variation-form of second-period style to the "invariant return" of the third)—to see in the imitative, contrapuntal, and intoxicating knowledge

---

8. Thomas Mann, *Doctor Faustus*, trans. H. Lowe-Porter (New York: Random House, 1966), pp. 242–43.

of music an allegory for the catastrophic collapse of a great civilizational achievement. Leverkühn's biography is the actualized form of this descent into the abyss, and it takes very little away from the concentrated power of Mann's novel that he does nothing less—as Rose Subotnik has shown—than convert Adorno's scattered philosophical ideas about the history of Western music into a consistent fable with an inexorably unchanging narrative direction.[9] The appropriate symbols for the two poles—the beginning in humanistic optimism and the ending in an anguished twelve-note dissonance—are Beethoven's "Ode to Joy" and the opening phrase of Berg's *Lulu*. The first, in its ringing affirmation of brotherhood and love, is the apotheosis of romantic possibility in which humankind embarks on great adventures with openness and cheer. The second is a dark concentration of an antihuman desperation; the notes suggest the depravity and alienation of a world, in Lukács's phrase, abandoned by God. Precisely because in its rebarbative complexity, without time or pleasing harmony, it can no longer serve as a reflection of human activity, music is a negation, a blotting-out of the society that gave rise to it.

As to whether in writing *Doctor Faustus* (or we, in reading it) Mann was right to press Adorno's severe and demanding negative dialectics either into the allegorical service he gets from it in his major novel—even if we allow for the common concern with modern catastrophe that Adorno shares with Mann—or into the systematic theorizations articulated by characters like Kretschmar or Adrian himself (but which Adorno resolutely seems to oppose everywhere else in his "anti-texts"), I am not entirely sure what the correct answer is. But Adorno himself suggests that the problematic of music's autonomy is, during the twentieth century, a matter not just of concern to specialists but of universal importance. Hence in *Philosophy of Modern Music* Adorno's powerful yet melodramatic characterizations of Schoenberg (unlike Stravinsky whose classicism Adorno abhors

9. See the opening pages of her essay "Adorno's Diagnosis of Beethoven's Late Style: Early Symptoms of Fatal Condition," *Journal of the American Musicological Society* 29 (Summer 1976).

as inauthentic and protofascist), who, like Leverkühn, comes to personify the weighty predicament of music's role in society. Thus it hardly matters in the end whether we criticize Mann and go back to Adorno, or use Adorno to understand Mann: the terms of discussion have largely been shut down by an overlapping theory of history and of music that relies on the occult, transgressive aspects of music to interpret history and, conversely, the deterministic and "objective" character of history to interpret music.

There is a genuinely interesting presentiment of the problems that this causes in the round table on *Doctor Faustus* held at Princeton in 1950 shortly after the novel appeared. Francis Fergusson, Joseph Kerman, E. T. O. Borgeroff, Erich Kahler, and Edmund King participated; the proceedings were chronicled by Robert Fitzgerald, who renders them memorably in his account of the 1949–51 Princeton Seminars, *Enlarging the Change.* On the one hand, Kahler was profoundly moved by the book's "high-strung, indeed rather overwrought, structural artistry in which not a single trait is left to playful divagation, but everything is strictly calculated in its correlation with everything else and with the whole—a combination . . . of such an almost mathematical artistry with an outburst of what he had carefully screened and disguised throughout his life."[10] On the other hand, Kerman found that the book was based on a false "master premise" (the antithesis between harmony and counterpoint), and that far from being justified Mann's "fantastic faith in history and fantastic distortion of it"[11] seriously flaw the book and its attempt to link compositional techniques with the *Zeitgeist.* There is a similar demurral at Mann's elisions in an intelligent essay on the novel by Robert Craft, who like Kerman is a musician and a critic.[12]

All retrospective historical analyses, whether of music or of

10. Robert Fitzgerald, *Enlarging the Change: The Princeton Seminars in Literary Criticism, 1949–1951* (Boston: Northeastern University Press, 1985), p. 181.
11. *Ibid.*, p. 195.
12. Robert Craft, "The *Doctor Faustus* Case," *New York Review of Books,* August 7, 1975.

any other human activity, that judge, theorize, and totalize simultaneously, that say in effect that one thing (like music) = all things, or all musics = one big summarizing result = it couldn't have happened any other way, seem to me to be intellectually and historically flawed, for the same reason that the later work of Foucault, to whom in all sorts of ways I am very indebted, is flawed. Recall that in *Surveiller et Punir* Foucault presents a breathtakingly powerful account of the emergence of various disciplines in modern Western European society at the beginning of the nineteenth century. He associates that emergence with the birth of prisons, hospitals, reform schools. By the end of the book he has begun to speak of how the microphysics of power that replaced the solitary power of the sovereign has achieved dominion over the whole of society, which he now calls a disciplinary society. One could say that Foucault was actually only making a theoretical statement, indifferent to whether it was in fact true or not, but we know from his own accounts of his political activities that for a time he was an energetic opponent of the disciplinary society: he engaged in agitation for prison reform in France, he was in regular contact with prisoners' groups, etc. Yet by the terms of the process he describes in *Surveiller et Punir* "the disciplinary society"—which bears a close resemblance to Adorno's "totally administered society"—has swept everything before it, including, as Nico Poulantzas was one of the first to note, all resistance to it.[13]

The point to be made here is that even if Foucault was correct (although to judge by his own activity he could not have been correct) there is very good reason for asking why the theoretical model abstractable from, or perhaps only imputable to, this account of the present (our "disciplinary society") should be so irresistibly total. Surely the various prison revolts, surely the

13. Nico Poulantzas, *L'Etat, le pouvoir, le socialisme* (Paris: Presses Universitaires de France, 1978), pp. 72–87. See also Said, "Foucault and the Imagination of Power," in *Foucault: A Critical Reader*, ed. David Couzens Hoy (Oxford: Basil Blackwell, 1986), pp. 149–55.

efforts of revolutionaries and reformers—for instance, the great slave rebellions that swept the French Caribbean colonies at the end of the eighteenth century, which led to the abolition of colonial slavery, and the abolitionist movement itself—these count for something in the narrative whose main focus is the unrelenting forward march of disciplinary society. Yet for Foucault, defiance, delinquency, criminality, and, in short, all forms of transgression serve two purposes: one, to be incorporated by the system, thereby confirming its power; two, to incriminate the system both for its inhumanity and for its inevitability.

It hardly needs saying that all of these immensely influential theories of cumulative and apocalyptic force—Thomas Mann, Foucault, Adorno, et al.—elevate admittedly discernible patterns in Western society during the modern period to the level of the essential and the universal. To call the theories therefore Eurocentric or imperial is, I believe, not an exaggeration, especially since in their combination of extreme detailed articulation, of self-reflective self-centeredness, of inevitabilism and aesthetic pessimism, they resemble each other in projecting no escape from, and no real alternative to, those patterns. Perry Anderson has quite rightly spoken of the combination of aestheticism and almost desperate pessimism that has afflicted the social theory of philosophers affiliated with what he has called Western Marxism.[14] And so, to bring in the de Man case one last time, the totalizing and overweening ideology that produced the habit of imposing murderous essentializations on Yeats's "uncontrollable mystery on the bestial floor" is not helpful in judging the moral, political, and cultural issue of what is essential to de Man's case, what is intrinsic to it, what extrinsic. In other words, we must be careful not to accept the assumption that in dealing with such issues in the case of Wagner, or de Man, or anyone else whose fate was tied in to the European apocalypse, that *that* was the only history, the only fate, the only culture and transgression worth thinking

14. Perry Anderson, *Considerations on Western Marxism* (London: New Left Books, 1976).

about. Not only must the resistance to fascism be given correlative attention, but so too must the dynamic of non-European history occurring simultaneously with events in Europe.

My contention is that considerations of music, art, and culture have therefore paid a very high price for these tremendous conflations, inflations, exaggerations. Consider the problem of essentialization, to which I alluded very quickly a moment ago. To say that questions that ask "What is music?" or "What is the literary, or literariness?" are impressively evident in recent discussions of art and politics is to say the obvious. What has needed saying, however, is that these same fascinated discussions, whose presence is so striking in Adorno, de Man, Wagner, etc., actually occur in a much wider framework than is usually allowed: namely, the tremendous imperial expansion of the West. For in the encounter between the West and its various "Others" (to employ a fashionable, but still useful word) there was often the tactic of drawing a defensive perimeter called "the West" around anything done by individual nations or persons who concentrated a self-appointed Western essence in themselves; this tactic protected against change and a supposed contamination brought forward threateningly by the very existence of the Other. In addition, such defensiveness permits a comforting retreat into an essentialized, basically unchanging Self. By the same token, there is a move to freeze the Other in a kind of basic objecthood.

This is not the place to survey the history of these moves and countermoves in detail. But it does bear saying that in addition to their commonly discussed significance Wagner and Mann also represent the crisis of modernism as it encounters for the first time a resurgent challenge from the Other, the Other not as inert object but as intrusive presence from outside the dominant metropolis; one can therefore note the parallel between Wagner's attacks (in the case of unregenerate outsiders like Beckmesser and Mime) on Jews and Mann's reaction to the Asiatic plague in *Death in Venice*, which disturbs the Apollonian, and very European, calm of Gustav von Aschenbach. Beyond these complicated engagements there are the great stirrings outside Europe provided by the forceful wars of independence and nationalist movements that later in the twentieth century will culminate in decolonization: this too encroaches upon European supremacy. To focus more narrowly upon what is purely European, or German, or French, or Jewish, or Indian, Black, Muslim, etc., is then to accept the very principle of a separate essentialization—the separation of the Jewish essence from the German, or the black from the white, etc.—and along with that to purify the types and to turn them into universals.

Such universals stand today as the legacy of the imperializing processes by which a dominant culture eliminated the impurities and hybrids that actually make up all cultures. Some sense of how important to contemporary history these processes are can be gleaned from a couple of recent studies, Martin Bernal's *Black Athena* and the various individual studies collected in *The Invention of Tradition*, edited by Eric Hobsbawm and Terence Ranger. Bernal's book chronicles the fabrication of a new "Aryan" classical antiquity at the end of the eighteenth century. Whereas the Greek texts themselves (as well as a millennium and a half of knowledge about ancient Greece) had acknowledged that Greece was in effect an Egyptian-African colony, generously influenced by Semitic civilization, the new European wish to purge Greece of its mixed non-European heritage, resulted in a rewriting of cultural history, the results of which are still with us. This virtually reconstituted and idealized "new" Attic Greece coincides with the emergence of classical philology as a profession, whose ideology—as Nietzsche was one of the first to make evident—required for its workings the manufacture of what Bernal calls a new model, an invasion from the North, to explain its origins. And this deliberately constructed paradigm was then elevated into a symbol, at once inviting and minatory, for the universal values of Western humanism.[15]

15. Martin Bernal, *Black Athena: The Afroasiatic Roots of Classic Civilization*, Vol. 1 ("The Fabrication of Ancient Greece 1785–1985") (New Brunswick: Rutgers University Press, 1987).

Much the same, but rather more social than intellectual, revamping of a messy actuality is described in *The Invention of Tradition*. The settings here are provided by modern colonial as well as metropolitan societies whose increasing social tensions (demographic, economic, political) dissolve old bonds, orthodoxies, and authorities and require the creation of imaginary structures that give new (but invented) continuity, permanence, and authority to ruling elites. Thus, for example, the ceremonies surrounding royalty, the mass public spectacles and festivals, the newly reedited histories that are so prominent a feature of modern India and Africa on the one hand, of Britain and the United States on the other, contribute to the way these societies are actually run.[16] To these examples we should add the equally charged case of racial thought as memorably described by Hannah Arendt in *The Origins of Totalitarianism*.[17]

All of what I have been discussing furnishes us with an apprehension of the global context for the kind of thinking about culture (and the place of music and literature in it) out of which Thomas Mann, among many others, made so much. To say that the horrors of totalitarianism came is to say what is undeniable about European history, but it is not to say everything about it, nor is it to say the only urgently relevant thing about world history in the twentieth century: there are other models for history, other efforts, other struggles equally worthy of study and reflection. What is especially important is that not *all* cultural or political endeavors were engulfed by the European avalanche, which while it did bring disasters to millions was neither the only aspect of history to have mattered nor the only one that should be returned to by specialized scholars and general intellectuals for counsel and instruction. In saying these things I intend no disparagement of anguished

16. Eric Hobsbawm and Terence Ranger, eds., *The Invention of Tradition* (Cambridge: Cambridge University Press, 1983), especially pp. 10–11 of Hobsbawm's "Introduction: Inventing Traditions."

17. Hannah Arendt, *The Origins of Totalitarianism* (1951; New York: Harcourt Brace, 1973), pp. 158–221.

and even bereaved efforts to understand the past and no derision whatever of thinkers like Adorno whose pessimistic brilliance and genuine profundity have dignified so much of contemporary intellectual discourse. I am saying, however, that a secular attitude warns us to beware of transforming the complexities of a many-stranded history into one large figure, or of elevating particular moments or monuments into universals. No social system, no historical vision, no theoretical totalization, no matter how powerful, can exhaust all the alternatives or practices that exist within its domain. There is always the possibility to transgress.

In its most literal sense transgression means to cross over, but rather than simply leave it at that I want to insist that the notion does not necessarily imply some irrevocable action against law or divinity. Secular transgression chiefly involves moving from one domain to another, the testing and challenging of limits, the mixing and intermingling of heterogeneities, cutting across expectations, providing unforeseen pleasures, discoveries, experiences. Once the totalizing tendency is refused an unquestioning assent, a whole series of transgressions both by and involving Western classical music proposes itself, and it is this I'd now like to consider.

Donald Francis Tovey makes the remark—quoting Albert Schweitzer—"that of all arts music is that in which perfection is a *sine qua non*."[18] Bach and Handel inaugurated what might be called perfection in practice. Much musicological and theoretical analysis is premised on this sort of *aperçu*, which gives rise to reverence, scholarship, and the like. Added to all these things is the very high degree of professionalization in musical discourse; this has had the effect of erecting a cordon around classical music as a cultural activity within society. Critics who have taken an interest in pop music—Jon Weiner and Simon Frith, most notably—have studied the ways in which the mass culture has commercialized and appropriated rock and jazz,

18. Donald Francis Tovey, *The Main Stream of Music and Other Essays* (New York: Meridian Books, 1959), p. 193.

even their most socially intransigent and resistant aspects. But things are quite different in what by common consent is considered the elite musical culture, at whose center stands a remarkable apparatus for producing and maintaining a discipline protected by rituals of learning, traditions of pedagogy, protocols of accreditation, performance, display, and so forth. Harmonic practice from the Baroque through the classical and early romantic period underwent numerous changes and shifts —compare a Haydn with a Chopin sonata and the contrast will be evident—but in effect a learned, extremely specialized language runs right through that period of almost a century and a half. To call this a police regime of the signifier is, I think, only a little to dramatize the extraordinary extent to which such a language is maintained in place and, conversely, the equally dramatic degree to which it seems to have forbidden, or at least partially prevented, encroachment or serious, perhaps even revolutionary, transformation.

And yet the performance, composition, and study of music has had remarkably persistent, if uneven and as yet unmapped, effects in Western society. The novelty now would be to think about these effects as an invasion by music into nonmusical realms, rather than the other way round. In other words, it is both interesting and novel to note that there have been consistent transgressions by music into adjoining domains—the family, school, class and sexual relations, nationalism, and even large public issues. A recent book by Jane Fulcher, *The Nation's Image,* subtitled *French Grand Opera as Politics and Politicized Art,* surveys programs at the main Paris opera theaters as they were influenced by and, more interestingly, an influence on national politics during the period 1830–70. Fulcher's conclusions are that there is a constant interplay among public spectacle, the types of emotions (such as patriotism, religious sentiment, romantic love) elicited by that spectacle, and such quotidian concerns as ticket prices, labor policies, crowd behavior, and larger political issues of moment such as government policy, public order, sedition, approval of specific laws, etc.[19]

A severer test of methodology and analysis is undertaken by Richard Leppert in *Music and Image: Domesticity, Ideology and Socio-Cultural Formation in Eighteenth-Century England*, where the site of musical practice that is excavated is domestic, the economy of the home, the relationship between men and women, between court, market, school. Leppert therefore works at the other—private or amateur—music-making end of the scale from Fulcher, although in Leppert's account of his subject the one motif that emerges with the clearest outline is authority and social control: music as enforcing class and gender divisions, music as deepening class differences, music as enhancing the prestige of male overlords.[20]

An even more recent work, Michael P. Steinberg's *The Meaning of the Salzburg Festival: Austria as Theater and Ideology, 1890–1938*, examines the role of Hugo von Hofmannsthal in establishing an annual festival in Salzburg at a time when the idea of Austria seemed particularly indistinct. Steinberg's analysis is both very detailed and subtle, and includes a considerable amount of material drawn from the history of Austrian anti-Semitism and assimilation, the ideology of the Baroque and Catholicism, and of course the particular careers of Viennese figures like Freud, Herzl, and von Hofmannsthal. But the interesting point here is that, according to Steinberg, Mozart's music was dragooned into cultural service "as the Kingpin of Salzburg's nationalist cosmopolitanism: the sharing of German culture with the outside world."[21] Therefore, his unredeemed hero, Don Giovanni, was recruited by the Salzburg festival

19. Jane Fulcher, *The Nation's Image: French Grand Opera as Politics and Politicized Art* (Cambridge: Cambridge University Press, 1987).

20. Richard Leppert, *Music and Image: Domesticity, Ideology and Socio-Cultural Formation in Eighteenth-Century England* (Cambridge: Cambridge University Press, 1988).

21. Michael P. Steinberg, *The Meaning of the Salzburg Festival: Austria as Theater and Ideology, 1890–1938* (Ithaca: Cornell University Press, 1990), p. 217.

impresarios to play alongside Hofmannsthal's *Jedermann* (his adaptation of *Everyman*), and *The Magic Flute* became "a natural common denominator for Salzburg's Mozart and baroque cults and Third Reich *volkisch* ideology."[22] Far from being the free-floating universal genius he has become since *Amadeus*, Mozart was right in the thick of cultural politics, as in fact his music has always been.

From the perspective of contemporary sociopolitical feminist concerns there are some important essays by Susan McClary on the contributions of music to the creation of problematic sexual stereotypes—effeminacy, exotic women (as in *Carmen*), victimizing man-eaters.[23] So impressive are the above-mentioned works by McClary, Leppert, Steinberg, and Fulcher, however, that they indicate a possible reason for the generally cloistral and reverential, not to say deeply insular, habits in writing about music. For the closer one looks at the geography of Western culture and of music's place in it, the more compromised, the more socially involved and active music seems, the more concealed its social energies have been beneath its technically specialized, rigorously circumscribed, and, since the seventeenth century, perfected articulations. If, for instance, we focus only on the schooling and channeling of romantic love and religious sentiment, music has played as generally significant a part as both literature and painting.

The association between Beethoven's *Fidelio* and an entire series of literary masterpieces extolling (but also ironizing) conjugal fidelity is considerable, yet few discussions of domestic narrative fiction have anything to say about *Fidelio*, any more than analyses of *Fidelio* include investigations of Alfred de Musset or Jane Austen. Similarly there are connections to be made between Isolde, Lulu, and Elektra on the one hand, and Nana, Eustacia Vye, and Molly Bloom on the other, connections that

---

22. *Ibid.*, p. 219.

23. In particular see her "Foreword" to Catherine Clément's *Opera, or the Undoing of Women*, trans. Betsy Wing (Minneapolis: University of Minnesota Press, 1988), pp. xi–xviii.

are far from adequately described as either earlier or later realistic (or decadent, or psychopathological) portraits of women. In all instances, as some younger scholars (Carolyn Abbate, Roger Parker, and others) have noted, the connections involve common formal, narratological, ideological, and psychological features both of literary and of musical styles. In other words, some of the valuable hints scattered here and there in the works of eminent musicologists (Dahlhaus, Cone, Meyer, Kerman, Gossett, Kivy, Taruskin, Treitler) normally focused on the specific character of music's social and aesthetic autonomy have now become a new area of musicological investigations, although I believe the institutionalized *pudeur* felt in regarding classical music as socially and culturally more than just "perfect" persists.

As indeed do the canonical structures, whether we think of general cultural analysis or of year-by-year performing repertory. Take, for example, symphonic and piano recital programs in a city like New York, which is regarded as one of the most important places to perform music, its concert and opera stages the locales of record. In opera the Metropolitan's repertory and style are fixed on a recurring group of three or four composers (Donizetti, Verdi, Puccini) and a dozen or so of their works, most of them falling comfortably within the *bel canto* or *verismo* categories. These have acquired a presence that has effectively blocked the performance of Czech, French, British, Russian, and most German opera, and has in turn encouraged the idea that opera is about overweight and disturbed people who sing unintelligibly and loudly. Similarly the symphonic and recital repertory is built around a classic Austro-Germanic set of composers (Mozart, Haydn, Beethoven, Brahms, Schumann, Bruckner, Mahler, etc.) that has either marginalized other composers and traditions (French, Czech, Spanish, Russian) or confined others to such degrading specialization as to turn their work into cliché. In this latter instance the fate of Chopin's work is egregious because he has survived not as the astonishing revolutionary he really was in all sorts of musical and cultural ways, but as a pianist's composer, at once effeminate and trivial. The word *salon* pretty much sums him up, especially in portentous discussions of Beethoven or Brahms.

No one is saying that canons do not in fact contain Arnoldian best-that-is-thought-or-said touchstones. Obviously they do, but what interests me about cultural canons and their consequences in general (or specifically musicological) analyses of music is that they tend to set limits and priorities too rigidly and too hierarchically. Too often as a result, the canon's eminence is associated with a sort of Darwinian or Hegelian inevitability, its laboriously constructed social authority either discounted or forgotten altogether. Moreover, the whole landscape in which canons belong is blotted out, leaving (to my mind) an unappealingly barren setting presided over by approved masterpieces and venerated authorities. We are therefore entitled to ask, "What happened to the elaborative work that put Beethoven where he is today, to the social formations that neglect Dussek and Hummel for Schubert and Brahms, to the intellectual effort that produced a Busoni, say, or a Boulez?"

Viewed as one of the rare self-consciously recapitulatory and summational moments in music, Wagner's *Die Meistersinger* therefore acquires a special meaning in light of these questions and considerations. Ideologically its conclusion is relatively straightforward, that German art in an ununified and politically incoherent patchwork of states can serve as an imagined community, to use Benedict Anderson's useful phrase. Yet the opera's enormous length argues for Wagner's sense of the need quite literally to work out, or elaborate, a set of social options for music—the opera is after all about musical composition, interpretation, and performance—otherwise left implicit in everyday musical activity or marginalized in the severely limited strictures legislated upon music externally and internally that culminate in Eduard Hanslick's *The Beautiful in Music*. The Meistersingers themselves are specified as artisans and as skilled musicians whose mastery of classical modes is made explicit to Walther in Act I by Fritz Kothner when he instructs him in the *Leges Tabulaturae*.

The genius of the opera is that Wagner shows how musical competence can mediate and cause adjustments to occur between the private world, with its impulses and drives like love, desire, jealousy, emulation, admiration, and the public sphere, constituted by the existence of a community presided over by a celibate sage (Hans Sachs) but also comprising youths, old people, artisans, apprentices, and miscellaneous townspeople. Few operas in my opinion have done so relentlessly detailed a job of literally enacting the way in which music, if it is looked at not simply as a private, esoteric possession but as a social activity, is interwoven with, and is important to, social reality. But what is fought for in *Die Meistersinger* is the song itself, music as symbolic of rewards and goods (Eva is perilously close to being a mere commodity) accruing to it only when it has crossed over from mere inspiration, or mere technical skill, into what is acceptable, agreed-upon, consensually granted. As for Wagner's neurotic closure whereby holy German art is affirmed in its foursquare establishmentarian virtue, we can take that as the merest crude attempt to grab once and for all what has already been proved to be a possession far in excess of, therefore transgressing, the clutches of one owner, be that owner an individual, town, or nation. Boulez is quite right to say that Wagner's "music by its very existence, refuses to bear the ideological message that it is intended to convey."[24] Read and heard for the bristling, tremendously energetic power of the *alternatives* to its own affirmative proclamations about the greatness of German art and culture, *Die Meistersinger* cannot really be reduced to the nationalist ideology its final strophes stress. It has set forth too much in the way of contrapuntal action, character, invention.

And because it belongs to the almost metamusical world of "opera and its inhabitants" as brilliantly discussed by Edward Cone,[25] its characters open to their own inner consciousness

24. Pierre Boulez, *Orientations: Collected Writings,* ed. Martin Cooper (London: Faber and Faber, 1986), p. 276.
25. Edward Cone, *Music, a View from Delft: Selected Essays,* ed. Robert P. Morgan (Chicago: University of Chicago Press, 1989), pp. 125–38.

with exceptional ease, *Die Meistersinger* is a contest for the very discourse or flowing lifeblood of music, which Wagner imagined as having already left the precincts of the hermetic and entered, crossed over and into, the social world. There it has become both acknowledged and realized, especially since "mastery" of music is for Walther, Sachs, and the whole of Nuremberg the key to bliss (with Woman as prize) and social authority. Doubtless the audacity and the length of the work reflect the ambition of its author, who had also become a political and cultural personality of more-than-local celebrity.

Measured against *The Magic Flute,* an important antecedent in the presentation of music's social role, *Die Meistersinger* has passed an important cultural milestone. Wagner's musicians are equally citizens and singers, breadwinners and aesthetic referees, the one quotidian life flowing naturally into the other, aesthetic one. Mozart's compression, his semaphoric allegorical style of connecting a sort of sublime simplicity with virtue, of associating virtuosic display with dangerous effeminacy, is a way, I think, of holding on to a shrinking domain, that of musician whose capital is his personal skill, hoarded against the terrifying impingements of worldly (largely nocturnal) temptations. Compare Sarastro's solemn (perhaps even parodistic) "In diesen heil'gen Hallen" with either of the two arias sung by the Queen of the Night and the point is painfully made. But whereas Sarastro and the Queen are only what they sing—the former a ponderously sublime cleric, the latter, not a character but an ephemeral and virtuosic machine for the display of feminine wiles—Wagner's personages appropriate each other's words and music because (as Cone puts it) for them the world of song and the world of everyday life supplement each other completely.[26]

But we should not drop the question of size and scale, which are such prominent features of Wagner's gigantically plotted and imagined music-dramas. Indeed, to a significant degree size and scale play a major role in the writing of composers

26. *Ibid.,* pp. 129–30.

since Beethoven, for whom the apparently classical limits of form required almost nonstop transgression in the direction of greater resources and length. In the *Poetics* Aristotle speaks of the drama as somehow possessing a necessary and proper magnitude or size, neither too large nor too small, neither too long nor too short. Out of this and other passages in the treatise there emerged the concept of classical unities, as well as notions of proportion, limit, and constraint that have long been associated generally speaking with Western art of the period up to 1800, after which extravagances of ego, sheer size, and massive effect become common. In music, we assume that modesty and impersonality are hallmarks of classical style; form is supposedly guided and informed by discreetness, whether in the sonata, in dance and aria forms, or in the various contrapuntal structures designed for multipurpose use in secular modes like opera and concerts, or religious modes like the mass, cantata, or motet.

These commonplaces have a kind of intuitive or immediate validity to them, and have often stamped the way we listen to Mozart and Haydn, for example, as opposed to Wagner and Strauss. The most generally well-received recent book on music is Charles Rosen's *The Classical Style*, the premises and conclusions of which are that classical style was a form of coherence gathered through a particular set of practices (Mozart, Haydn, Beethoven) that acquired an idiomatic equipoise summoning such elements as harmony, ornament, structure, and sonata form to overall collective use. Yet by the end of the book in a section on Beethoven, Rosen is compelled to discuss such works as the *Hammerklavier* Sonata, the *Grosse Fuge*, and *An die ferne Geliebte* as stepping "outside the classical aesthetic."[27] Other commentators on Beethoven (notably Maynard Solomon and Wilfrid Mellers)[28] have also tried to deal with Beethoven's repeated assaults on the discretion inherent in musical form that

27. Charles Rosen, *The Classical Style: Haydn, Mozart, Beethoven* (New York: Viking, 1971), p. 402.
28. Wilfrid Mellers, *Beethoven and the Voice of God* (London: Faber and Faber, 1983); Maynard Solomon, *Beethoven* (New York: Schirmer Books, 1977).

he inherits from Mozart and Haydn; their themes are—here I again paraphrase crudely—that Beethoven's strivings for extreme types of expression represent pioneering modes of thought about new "psychic and social experience," and that his late style, with its "aggressive, dotted-rhythmic polyphonic textures . . . creates a simultaneous sense of irresistible motion and unbearable strain."[29]

What appears to me to be no less the case is that Beethoven's music, in contrast to the works of Mozart, Bach, and Handel, signals a dramatically new way of understanding the importance of elaboration, its working out and filling of time and social space. The ceremonies of power and reverence enabling Bach's choral works, for instance, are entirely provided beforehand; his music was to fill in, to contribute to, the enhancements of adulation due to princes and bishops, who were easily seen not only as worldly patrons but as earthly representatives of the divine. A work like the B Minor Mass is an astonishing demonstration of piety and invention, but for all the intensity and skill of its various parts—unprecedented before 1733, the year of its performance—it must also be read as an extended act of homage to the Elector of Saxony, to whom Bach addressed the most fawning letters imaginable. Thus the unclassical length of the piece derives not just from Bach's genuinely extraordinary authorial productivity, which has been too easily reified and romanticized by generations of humanists and musicologists, but from the ambition to win a place of noticeable importance in the entourage of a prince. Music therefore quite literally fills a social space, and it does so by elaborating the ideas of authority and social hierarchy directly connected to a dominant establishment imagined as actually presiding over the work. The awe we feel in the Credo, for example, reinforces the separation between ruler and ruled, and this in turn is made to feel "right" in great outbursts of joy ("et resurrexit," and "hosanna"). Not enough of this has been studied as giving

29. Maynard Solomon, *Beethoven Essays* (Cambridge, Mass.: Harvard University Press, 1988), p. 296.

a particular social presence to Bach's music, since what is generally current in writing about music today is tied to (when it is not actually constituted by) the idea that music has an apolitical and asocial autonomy.

After noting these transgressions from the purely musical to the social in Bach and Handel (who has a much more jaunty and even careless attitude to his own work as a result of his self-consciousness about his social role), it is not taking an enormous step to examine the institutionalized concerts and festivals that overtake their bigger works in the mid-nineteenth century. Here the filling of leisure time by undertaking a week of Bach and Handel festivals (Wagner understood this perfectly of course) was not only an unclassical practice, it was positively middle class: a concentration of major works played *seriatim* as a way of using unexpended time, as well as a way the official culture had of celebrating itself.[30] Music has crossed over further into a province held apart for the cultural masterpieces designated by Matthew Arnold, that roster of monuments considered to be above controversy and gross politics. That these literary monuments and musical works like them are in fact saturated with some form or other of politics—for example, Berlioz's *Les Troyens* (1860) in the French conquest of North Africa, or Verdi's *Aida* (1870)[31] in the European domination of the Near East, or the various Austrian and French works discussed by Jane Fulcher and Michael Steinberg: the list is almost infinitely extendable—is rarely broached in musical analyses, perhaps for fear that too close a look would itself be a form of intolerable transgression, and certainly a loss of the autonomy conferred upon classical music.

Beethoven's revolution in music was almost single-handedly to shift the basis of compositional time from semiofficial designations provided by rulers, church feasts, ceremonies, to the far more precarious and novel space opened up by the tonal

30. I discuss this phenomenon in *The Nation*, August 30, 1986, pp. 150–53.

31. See my discussion of *Aida* in "The Imperial Spectacle (*Aida*)," *Grand Street* 6, 2 (Winter 1987): 82–104.

system and its rudimentary cadences, which the composer can then proceed to exploit first by sheer rude insistence, then later by self-dramatization, then finally by a radical reexploration of the system itself. Here we should look principally not at the beginnings of Beethoven's works (they are almost always either atmospheric, as in the various "Leonore" overtures, the *Pastoral* Symphony, the Choral Fantasy, or harmonically suggestive and motivically enunciatory, as in the First, Second, *Eroica*, and Fifth symphonies) but at their endings. The Fifth Symphony is a perfect case in point, with its relentless tonic-dominant pattern giving way to a veritable tumult of C-major chords: Beethoven saying, in effect, C major is mine, I close the space I have explored with the chord and by virtue of that key, again, again, again, it is mine, mine, mine. There is primitive hoarding here (an echo of this turns up in the C-major chords associated not only with Wagner's Rhinegold motif but even with the insolent hammering motifs that dominate *Das Rheingold*, scene 3, and *Siegfried*, Act One) and the statement of a new fact (Example 6).

By the time of Brahms and Bruckner musical elaboration has been given a more solid, more assured, less strident texture. Duration is much less frenetic and rushed, there is a greater sense of the composer's egoistical privilege, a deeper awareness, especially in Brahms, of abstract—because socially marginalized and confined to the safe space of the concert hall—patterns and formulas that cannot long sustain inspired eloquence (of the sort Beethoven concentrated in his middle-period slow movements), introspection, and self-assertion as they did for a beginner like Beethoven. The world of patronage is now separately capitalized, as represented by the concert occasion and the publisher, and the place of music in the social narrative has become largely meditative, self-referential, and decorative. It is against this demeaning reality that Wagner's narratives react in the *Ring* (see especially *Die Walküre*, Act II; *Siegfried*, Act I; *Götterdämmerung*, Act I). Unable to accept the subsidiary role to which music has been condemned, Wagner resists, all the while revealing how insecure his social place really is.

For despite its inhumanly remorseless forward progress (in which in some ways it resembles a Dickens or Balzac novel), the *Ring* is really a work about slipping and going backwards, and was never really fully completed. Wagner began with the death of Siegfried, and worked his way back to the origin of all things in the Rhine. Only then did he impose on his tetralogy the step-by-step march to annihilation, the reassertion of redemptive love, the disappearance of the old order. Unlike the Attic tragedians that he emulated, however, Wagner had no social or political community on which he could depend for the cathartic rejuvenations of the whole society such as take place at the end of the *Oresteia* or the Theban plays; he had to provide everything himself, from out of his ego, his universal art work, his Kingdom at Bayreuth. Thus he was always *redoing* things, restructuring, repairing, reinterpreting in an effort to get them right and give them stability *as if* from the beginning. This is why the *Ring* is full of characters who, like Wagner, tell the story over and over again.

These recitations are direct evidence of how Wagner's central impulse is a sort of desperate narrative that attempts to bring order and rest to a world that is beset, like Emma Bovary's, with creditors and spiteful gossips. Each of the stories told by nearly every character in the cycle—the Rhinemaidens, Loge, Erda, Siegmund, etc.—jostles the others, claiming attention and space, the whole contained by the orchestra, which is the narrative-of-all-narratives. It is this profusion of warring tales and power-driven characters that symbolizes the seething instability lodged at the *Ring*'s center, despite the work's outer solidity and imposing bulk. Produce dreams *and* power, hold on to as much as you can, try to dominate others: this is the *Ring*'s irreducible core, embodied in the exploits of Alberich, Wotan, Hunding, Hagen, Siegfried and even the dwarf Mime. Each such career, like a line of music, inevitably gives rise to others. Since the contest between them can never be resolved,

EXAMPLE 6. Beethoven's Symphony No. 5 in C Minor, closing measures of fourth movement

it can only be restaged again and again, much as the pursuit of power and capital is an everlasting effort. Wagner fully realized the remarkable parallel between the development of symphonic music and the development of a competitive bourgeois society and used the *Ring* in effect to stage, or embody, and contain the parallel. But in addition, the *Ring* tetralogy, *Die Meistersinger*, and *Parsifal*—he spoke once of "deeds of music made visible"—attempted quite self-consciously to produce an alternative discourse for a civil society that had excluded Wagner and forced him to set up his own society in Bayreuth; in it, and on a stage quite literally his, he can tell his own stories, embroider and interpret them, tell them over and over.

None of what I have said can possibly imply therefore that the affiliations between music and society—what I have been calling transgression—reduce music to a subordinate, passively mirroring role. On the contrary, music plays a role in civil society that is neither natural nor substitutive. Music is of course *itself,* even if its way of inhabiting the social landscape varies so much as to affect compositional and formal styles with a force as yet largely uninventoried in cultural studies now. In short, the transgressive element in music is its nomadic ability to attach itself to, and become a part of, social formations, to vary its articulations and rhetoric depending on the occasion as well as the audience, plus the power and the gender situations in which it takes place. In this respect Western classical music in particular can usefully be regarded as one of the products of intellectual labor that Gramsci analyzed as constituting what he called the "elaboration" of Western civil society. Seen in this slightly alienating way, music shares a common history of intellectual labor with the society of which it forms so interesting and engaging an organic part. Thus we can see musicians as belonging to the intellectual class even though they are a distinct subgroup, with their own procedures, associations, powers, and standards. Their contribution today is to the maintenance of society, giving it rhetorical, social, and inflectional identity through composition, performance, interpretation, scholarship, and, yes, a kind of professionalism that removes and to a degree isolates music in an apparently idealized domain of its own.

But all we need to do is to look at the whole field of classical music as a mode of dominance in sustaining the structure of the status quo, or in its fate as a field of human endeavor challenged from time to time by other cultures, other nonelite formations, alternative subcultures, to grasp something of the whole social contest in which music is often involved. To think of music and cultural exoticism in the mid to late nineteenth century (Verdi, Bizet, Wagner, Saint-Saëns, etc.) or of music and politics during the seventeenth and twentieth centuries (Monteverdi, Schoenberg, jazz, and rock culture) is therefore to map an ensemble of political and social involvements, affiliations, transgressions, none of which is easily reducible either to simple apartness or to a reflection of coarse reality.

If that is so we should also be able finally to locate and identify a relatively rare number of works making (or trying to make) their claims entirely *as music,* free of many of the harassing, intrusive, and socially tyrannical pressures that have limited musicians to their customary social role as upholders of things *as they are.* I want to suggest that this handful of works expresses a very eccentric kind of transgression, that is, music being reclaimed by uncommon, and perhaps even excessive, displays of technique whose net effect is not only to render the music socially superfluous and useless—to *discharge* it completely—but to recuperate the craft entirely for the musician as an act of freedom. *Così fan tutte* can, I think, be read that way as a whole, its radical amorality and supernal elegance cutting right across the tidy little conventions of eighteenth-century court theater; no one is spared Mozart's coruscating irony, and no declaration or quasi-philosophical observation does not turn back on its speaker. What remains, then, is a sort of canceled philosophical statement about conjugal fidelity leaving behind it a musical statement, as William Mann puts it well, of "brilliant variety, cocky, martial, sad, astonished, angry."[32]

A still more phenomenal example is the keyboard work by Bach known as the "Canonic Variations" on *Von Himmel hoch*. Written late in his life, it is ostensibly a series of embellished settings of a very familiar Christmas chorale. In fact, it is an exercise in pure combinatorial virtuosity. The melody is set first in the bass, then in the soprano, then in middle voices, all the time that the figural elaborations imitate each other in strict canon writing at different chordal intervals. Yet the overall impression communicated by the work is of something plastic and benign: the fiercesomely problematic contrapuntal difficulties negotiated by Bach are, as it were, completely disguised. Moreover, the chorale melody itself is displaced so often from one register to the other that we sense Bach's ability to dislodge even the chorale's pious technical sententiousness with polyphonic manipulations that testify to a demonic power. One will have to wait until Webern's *Variations* to get something so formidably, concentratedly articulated as this music, but so far in excess is it of any occasion or need that it dangles pretty much as pure musicality in a social space off the edge.

32. William Mann, *The Operas of Mozart* (New York: Oxford University Press, 1979), p. 556.

# Melody, Solitude, and Affirmation

Most readers of Marcel Proust are impressed with the stunning passages on music that dot *A la recherche du temps perdu*, so it must come as a considerable surprise to the nonprofessional reader and admirer of Proust that neither "la petite phrase de Vinteuil" nor Vinteuil's Septet has ever really been identified as a piece of real music, much less heard. An interesting book, *Proust musicien*, by the French Canadian musicologist Jean-Jacques Nattiez (also the author of a noteworthy book on the 1976 Boulez-Chérau *Ring* production), argues in detail what has always seemed to me a very convincing thesis, that music plays perhaps the single most important formative and shaping role of any art in Proust's novel. Nattiez traces much of Proust's passion for music to an inaugural period in his planning for *A la recherche*, a time when he seems to have come under the spell of Wagner's "Good Friday" music for *Parsifal*. Thereafter, Nattiez says, Wagner and Vinteuil support each other in Proust's mind. Like Proust himself, both master-musicians are determined to find the essence of things in music; both are influenced by Schopenhauer, and the two musicians, one actual, the other a fictional creation, as well as Proust himself, believed that human redemption could occur in and through a work of art.

Nattiez is certainly right in saying that no writer devoted as much and as qualitatively significant a portion of his or her work to descriptions of music as Proust did.[1] Not even the casual reader of Proust can ever forget the tremendously affecting passage on Vinteuil's Septet in *La Prisonnière*, performed at a special Verdurin evening, in that this one unites the worldly group of Charlus, Morel, Vinteuil's daughter, and of course the narrator, who is reminded of his love for Albertine; in *Swann's Way* a Verdurin evening had earlier provided a perhaps less complicated group with notable aesthetic pleasures, also the result of a composition by Vinteuil. On both these musical occasions performance is what gives rise to Proust's meditations on life, art, love, eternity, and redemption. For music, like Proust's major theme in his work, is based on time, or rather on an experience of the passing of time through which, as Marcel says in *La Prisonnière*, the listener is led "de trouvaille en trouvaille."[2]

Yet Time in Proust is in the first instance, and thereafter through recollection, bound to actual material reality; part of the pathos of these extraordinary moments of transcendence in *Le Temps retrouvé* is Marcel's recollection not just of past experiences but of the very object in which experience seems to be lodged, like that particular copy of *François le champi* Marcel read in his little room in Combray ("pendant la nuit peut-être la plus douce et la plus triste de ma vie"),[3] and which in turn gave rise to similar experiences separated from it in time. Yet Marcel also describes how such objects acquire an immaterial existence when they mix indissolubly—the word is Proust's— into the general mixture of other thoughts and sensations of

1. Jean-Jacques Nattiez, *Proust musicien* (Paris: Christian Bourgois, 1984), pp. 35 and following.
2. Marcel Proust, *A la recherche du temps perdu*, Vol. III (Paris: Gallimard, 1954), p. 154.
3. *Ibid.*, p. 886.

that time. Thus, he says, a name read in a book "contient entre ses syllabes le vent rapide et le soleil brillant qu'il faisait quand nous le lisions."[4]

What Proust repeatedly underlines throughout is the individuality of the work, the artist, and the auditor, reader, or spectator. Because of its muteness music involves even deeper problems of understanding and, as Antoine Compagnon sensitively points out in a recent study, it is Proust's special regard for Wagner that elicits that combination of enthusiasm and judgment characterizing his view of the great German musician and iconoclastic mythographer.[5] And this attitude confirms the precarious singularity that so eminently attaches to the uniqueness of music itself. It is Wagner after all who for Proust raises the whole question of whether the greatest nineteenth- century art works (*La Comedie humaine, La Legende des siècles, La Bible de l'humanité* are also mentioned) are not in reality fundamentally incomplete, to be given their unity by acts of what Proust calls *illumination retrospective*. What if, as he seems to believe was the case with Wagner, musical composition was based on fits of inspired enthusiasm interspersed with a forgetfulness that is later dispelled by renewed recollection (Proust's example is the shepherd's air in *Tristan*)? Proust speaks in wonderful phrases of "l'allegresse du fabricateur" and of his "habileté vulcanienne," that slightly disappointing almost alchemical skill in improvising illusions of aesthetic unity that splendid figures such as Wagner possess in profusion.

When a moment later Marcel adds that all his musical experiences ultimately come back to the great performances of his time he has added yet another individualizing trait to the series that begins with the artist's conceiving mind. Music is of fundamental interest therefore because it represents the rarity, uniqueness, and absolute individuality of art, as well as its intermittent, fragmentary, highly conditional, and circumstantial existence. When we hear or experience music through per-

4. *Ibid.*, p. 885.
5. Antoine Compagnon, *Proust entre deux siècles* (Paris: Seuil, 1989), pp. 36–52.

formance we are moreover compelled to a rigorous linear attention by the sheer unfolding quality in time of the music. True,
certain sonorities, moments, and passages stand out and, like
the Vinteuil passage that recurs in *Swann's Way*, acquire an
almost independent life of their own. But even they, in their
supremely individualistic and completely unusual essence, are
to some degree commanded by passing time. To know a piece
of music, then, is always to acknowledge the ineluctable temporal modality, or one-timeness, of the audible; you cannot
experience it, as you can, say, when you pause before or walk
around a painting or a sculpture, without also submitting to
the tyranny of its forward logic or impulse.

Thus even though the one-time occasion or performance of
music is a central aspect of musical life, one can always return
to these occasions through memory, as Proust's eloquent pages
so amply attest. Yet Proust's recurrences inevitably point away
from the public aspects of an occasion—sitting in a concert hall
or salon, for instance—to its private possibilities; for example,
the recollection, often shared, often lonely, of pains, anguish,
bodies, miscellaneous as well as musical sounds, and so on. I
find this characteristic tendency in Proust very moving, obviously because in its poignancy and psychological richness it
has helped me to comprehend a great deal about my own
experiences of music, experiences that seem to me like an un-
ceasing shuttle between playing and listening privately for myself and playing and listening in a social setting, a setting
whose constraints and often harsh limitations (for example, the
dreary sameness of most concerts, the failing capacities of hand,
eye, memory, and mind that come with age, the comic, entirely
parodistic familiarity with what Adorno calls "alienated masterpieces" enabled by record players and electronic gadgets) only
suddenly and very rarely produce so novel, so intense, so
individualized, and so irreducible an experience of music as to
make it possible for one to see it in a lot of its richness and
complexity almost for the first time.

But then that occasion in its uniqueness becomes extendable

EXAMPLE 7. Brahms, Theme with Variations for Piano

EXAMPLE 8. Brahms, Sextet No. 1

through repeated, although intermittent, experiences with the music. A few years ago Alfred Brendel gave a Carnegie Hall recital whose contents were made up exclusively of pieces based on a theme-and-variation pattern. The climax was to be constituted by Beethoven's *Diabelli* Variations, although the three preceding works—by Mozart, Brahms, and Liszt—were obviously substantial and in their own ways just as interesting. Only the Brahms had me somewhat perplexed since I have a poor memory for opus numbers (this one was opus 18) and I could not place this particular set of variations. After a little investigation I discovered that the program notes identified the piece as dedicated to Clara Schumann and taken from the String Sextet in B flat. Until Brendel began to play the variations I still had not—for completely nonmusical and accidental reasons—grasped what exactly they were; when he did play them, the unexpected pleasure of recognizing the piece from a different context, its original string version, quickly took over, though as he played I was conscious of trying to compare the transcription (Example 7) with the chamber ensemble score with which I am familiar (Example 8).

They tallied exactly. I later discovered in an essay by Donald Francis Tovey that Brahms played the piece quite frequently in recitals he gave later in his life,[6] perhaps—I speculated—as an

6. Donald Francis Tovey, *The Main Stream of Music and Other Essays* (New York: Meridian Books, 1959), p. 231.

act of remembrance and homage to Clara whom he had apparently always loved but from whom he always maintained a perplexed and poignant distance after Schumann's death in 1856. Brendel's performance was therefore significant to me because it made me unusually attentive. This was not like his performances of the Mozart variations on a theme of M. Duport, which I know very well, or the much grander *Diabelli* and the Liszt variations on Bach's "Weinen, Klagen, Sorgen, Zagen," which I also know and have heard performed several times. In the *Diabelli* Variations he was, I thought, exceptionally sharp, playing right up to the edge of the notes, fleetly, perceptively, intelligently, especially in those variations where one could hear Beethoven's lively humor and often coarse wit alternating with the elegant and meditative zeal with which in the last three variations he saluted Bach and Handel, at the same time as he drew from the spirited little theme almost grotesque embellishments and elaborations.

Because of its familiarity, I could think about and analyze most of Brendel's program as I listened. This was not the case with the Brahms, in which, as I mentioned, I was following along almost literally, going over the notes with Brendel as the score unfolded during performance. Strangely, I think the effort of correspondence held me much more rigorously to the music than is usually the case: I assimilated, I actively bound my hearing to, an earlier but still lively experience of the score with Brendel's performance, and Brendel in turn was seeking to tie himself to the music physically and intellectually, on the assumption that Brahms had been attempting to do the same with reference to his own original string version.

But this was not all, for underlying the pleasure of these fulfilled conjunctions was another series of feelings, no less held in place by the uncommonly strict, even though lyrical and austerely sentimental, character of the variations. I should say that Brahms's music has always been a problem for me as much because large stretches in his writing (the choral, vocal, and some piano music is especially vulnerable here) contain expert yet unrewarding complexity, as because other pieces—

the Haydn and Handel variations, the Second and Fourth symphonies, the violin and cello sonatas, the B major trio—are so
compellingly, hauntingly right for me as I listen to or play
them. Brahms's sweetness, which is sometimes derided in fa-
vor of the rhetorical ponderousness of his solemn music like
the *Requiem* and the *Alto Rhapsody*, is remarkably successful
because it appears surrounded by forbiddingly dense writing;
the contrast is breathtaking, for example, if we juxtapose the
(to me) noisy arridity, dutifully thumped out by many orches-
tras season after season, of the First Symphony with the unas-
suming D major of the Second, especially after an unpromising
four-note growl (D–C-sharp–D–A) in the opening measures is

EXAMPLE 9. Brahms, Symphony No. 2, extract from first movement

immediately answered by the horns and bassoons (Example 9).

The D-major realization in the succession from measures one to two and three is, without giving it a technical designation, satisfying and affirmative, and it seems to confirm some plan to move and develop the music that Brahms does not always have when he is taking on the role, exaggerated by perhaps thinking of himself as a successor to Beethoven, of serious (yet often only divagating and maundering but ever so earnest) Kapellmeister.

The variations played by Brendel are extracted by Brahms from a theme that, certainly compared to the Duport (Example 10) and Diabelli themes (Example 11), is rich in many ways: it is declamatory, confident, intimate, and yet self-exposing, es-

EXAMPLE 10. Mozart, *Duport* Variations

EXAMPLE 11. Beethoven, *Diabelli* Variations

pecially dramatic in the alternation between major and minor modes.

The fourth variation is one of two variations in D major (there are five variations in all). It too has a sort of affirmative and fulfilled character, stating the original D-minor theme in D major over a running hymnlike bass line that at first doubles the soprano and alto themes but then is deployed against them through the use of descending octaves, which are opposed to the theme's generally rising character (Example 12). Listening to it in Carnegie Hall I was reminded spontaneously of the "Nimrod" variation in Elgar's *Enigma* Variations, which I had heard played a few days before by the Montreal Symphony under Charles Dutoit. According to his program for the piece, Elgar's wish for his work was to evoke a set of his friends in various rural English settings. There is an emphatically expansive, serene, even assuredly satisfied E-flat broadness to "Nimrod" that is similar to what Brahms also communicates in the D-major of variation four (Example 13).

Variation four seemed to me also to play a unifying, summarizing role in the piece as a whole. Brahms restates a com-

EXAMPLE 12. Brahms, Theme with Variations for Piano, fourth variation

pact version of the theme in major, removes from it its insistent
and imprecatory strummed accompaniment, and lets it sing
forth with the only breaks added for rhetorical emphasis in the
melody line provided by the ornamental turns, which have
always fascinated me in classical and romantic music. These
turns work as a kind of melodic underlining, in which extra
syllables and a decorative link between one segment of the line

EXAMPLE 13. Elgar, *Enigma* Variations, "Nimrod"

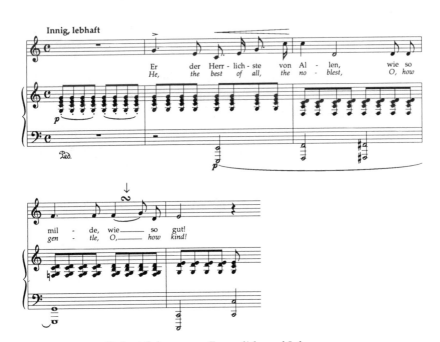

EXAMPLE 14. Robert Schumann, *Frauenliebe und Leben*

and another are employed; and yet to me these basically conventional ornaments manage somehow to communicate a
speechless, contentless eloquence I find very difficult to explain. Here is one such example in a song from Schumann's
*Frauenliebe und Leben* (Example 14). No: it is not just eloquence
and a certain quasi-chivalric courtliness; in the turn at the words
"wie so gut" there is, inexplicably, pathos and a sense of loss.
Wagner makes wonderful use of the turn in *Tristan* (Example
15), but so too does Strauss—for example, in *Capriccio* (Example 16). If the ornament is not executed with absolute cor-
rectness it can sound highly jolly, and of course supremely
pointless.

As Brendel played the fourth variation, two other versions
of the Sextet came to mind, or rather came to find a place for
themselves in the music now so single-mindedly being put
forward by the pianist. One was the old Prades festival recording in which Pablo Casals takes so unmistakably commanding
a role; the ensemble isn't less an ensemble for its submission to
his will, since he exercises his power, paradoxically, with non-
coercive authority. I have not heard the piece in that version
for at least twenty years, but I remember clearly both his soar-
ing line in the fourth variation and his (as I remember) audible
breathing and humming. And that memory led me back to
Louis Malle's film *Les amants*, constructed around the relatively
innocuous tale of a nameless unknown man happening on a
lonely wife (Jeanne Moreau) in the country, and then becoming
her lover for a time before he moves on. Malle had used the
variation movement of the Brahms Sextet as the chief element
in the film's scoring.

I do not want to add here an inventory of the fleeting, often
banal nonmusical associations that came to mind as I listened
to Brendel. They were and are there, but I would find it hard
to list them since, as they occurred *because* of the music, they
seemed to have only a secondary, derivative cogency to them;
they were numerous as well as indistinct, and more to the
point, they occurred in the genre of subordinate, literally incon-
sequential irrelevancies. What made the whole experience I am

EXAMPLE 15. Wagner, *Tristan und Isolde*

describing especially noteworthy was that I later quite easily found the variations in a volume of Brahms's piano music, and have since spent a fair time playing—not practicing, but playing—them through. I had not heard any recording of the piano piece until well over a year after I had heard it performed by Brendel.

EXAMPLE 16. Richard Strauss, *Capriccio*

I have gone to such length to try to characterize a relatively personal experience of conventional Western classical music in order to register how a set of disparate things coming together consolidate and affirmatively support each other. As against those occurrences there are what Proust so precisely depicted as the ravagements of quotidian life, those dangerous solvents of the aesthetic experiences that we treasure, those pressures that render "les intermittences du coeur" so regrettably fleeting and scarce. I would not go so far as to say that the various reinscriptions of the Brahms variations had the effect for me of something objective; rather I would say that the music itself was affirmed for me, no doubt much of it, as Gramsci would say, in a muscular-nervous way, because I was able a short time after Brendel's recital to play it on the piano. That particular physical discipline anchored the other convergences of memory and intellectual history in a practice that was also a discipline of detail: for you cannot play, at least on my level of piano technique, without an almost total absorption in the notes, as they require you rigorously to coordinate your fingers with the intellectual decoding of the score. In addition, you must also attend minutely to phrasing, tempo markings, dynamics, rhetoric, and anagogies or inflections in the rhythmical pulse.

Let me go a bit further. It is quite easy to remark on the analogies between good reader-critics of literature and good reader-critics, that is, performers, of music. In all these discussions, however, we should note the useful working distinction between composing and interpreting, or between creating a text and re-creating it. This is a distinction, however, that should not become rigid or so hard and fast as to separate completely related activities. What interests me is the way the best interpreters of poetry and music allow both their audience and themselves (self-conviction being not the least of the interpreter's virtues) the proposition that the work being presented is *as if* created by the performer. Somehow the work appears to gain its justification, its rightness, its *thereness* in the words of Sergiu Celibidache, by that interpretation. You understand how the specific work of music originally came about, even though the mode of the work's interpretative presentation—the critical essay or the actual performance, which in some aspects can quite easily be compared with an essay—is different from the composer's, but is almost of coeval interest and worth.[7] So performance of a work of music aims at identity: between interpretation and the work, between performer and listener, between this particular work and other related works, and so forth. Because the work unfolds in, indeed is irrecusably tied to, duration or passing time, it can be listened to as if (the phrase is meant to underline the provisionality of the experience) from the point of view of its creator, as if he or she was composing it during that time. This is of course an illusion.

There are all sorts of variants on this idea. Performers and interpreters can quite validly present the work antagonistically or antithetically, but even there we sense some actual informing identity enabling the criticism or antagonism, another performance, another composer, another author or critic. For example, some years ago Maurizio Pollini presented a Carnegie Hall recital composed entirely of Book I of Bach's *Well-Tempered Clavier*. So long and formidable a program, played by so fa-

---

7. I have discussed these notions, as well as Pollini's performance of Bach (discussed in the following paragraph), in "Remembrance of Things Played: Presence and Memory in the Pianist Is Art," *Harper's*, November 1985, pp. 69–75.

mous and prodigiously endowed a pianist (not known as a Bach specialist), ended up by making an unmistakable statement that, in this case, seemed to address itself to the one other recent pianist who played Bach, Glenn Gould. Pollini's playing seemed to say that his was meant to be as *unlike* Gould's as possible, and identified itself instead with the playing of Ferruccio Busoni, the great Italian pianist of an earlier generation who also was known as a Bach specialist. Such references and allusions, negative and positive, create the context of musical presentation and representation, and they also enforce or deemphasize commitments to individual style, period, or composers.

So in the case of the Brahms variations I found myself playing them with (for me) an unusual commitment to Brahms's music, in part because as I played I found myself recollecting with poignant nostalgia the voice and even the pianistic gestures of an old teacher, Ignace Tiegerman, a Polish Jew who had come to Egypt (which is where I met him in the 1950s) after he had discovered the impending portent of fascism for him as a European musician and performer during the 1930s. He had been a Wunderkind pupil of Theodor Leschetizky contemporaneously with Artur Schnabel in Berlin (in 1911 I believe), and later went on to study with one of Leschetizky's most gifted disciples, Ignace Friedman.

Tiegerman was a remarkable phenomenon. In part, I think, his extraordinary gifts were accentuated for me because of how they clashed with the anomalous background provided by Cairo, where he stood out as a tiny, almost dwarflike and sharp-featured creature with a marked Polish accent and trilingual facility in hybrid versions of French, German, and English (no Arabic at all), imperious in his ways, heedless and yet occasionally apprehensive about the massive political changes in Egypt as it went from its Faroukian degeneracy into the assertive triumphalism of its Arab nationalist phase under Gamal Abdel Nasser. Tiegerman was a profoundly, but attractively, lazy man who ran a conservatory and employed piano and violin teach-

ers with a kind of salonlike languor.[8] He himself was a mercu-
rial teacher, but certainly the most musical and ingenious that I
ever encountered. His own playing controlled the entire repertory roughly speaking, from the middle-period Beethoven war-
horses (for example, the *Appassionata* and *Waldstein* sonatas)
through to Liszt, Chopin, Schumann, Brahms, plus a handful
of twentieth- century works by Rachmaninoff, Szymanowski,
and Prokofiev. As I played the Brahms D Minor Variations I
found myself recalling—I mean the word literally—Tiegerman's playing of the Brahms D Minor Piano Concerto, in which,
as he once said, the difficulty was to separate the actual music
from the large mass of the score's many notes. I remember
asking him then whether he "really" liked Brahms, my tone
indicating the perhaps jejune doubts and vacillations about
Brahms that I felt even as he played the piece so convincingly.
Yes, he said, but only if you really *know* about him, nodding at
his hands as he played.

This wasn't connoisseurship or blasé familiarity. It suggested
a whole tradition of teaching and playing that entered into and
formed my own relationship with Tiegerman, as it must have
between him and his colleagues and friends in Europe. Out of
that emerged a capacity for giving life to a piece *in* the performance, a capacity dependent on knowing a composer through
a structure of feeling—I borrow here from Raymond Williams
—that is apparent only when one goes through the detailed
articulation of the work; this articulation cannot exist without,
and indeed relies on, the official corpus of canonical music, its
formalities, rules, structures, and styles, but in effect it exists
beyond the canon.[9] This is by no means a capacity and a
knowledge equivalent to musicological expertise or what Adorno
calls structural listening, though I assume that such formal and

8. I have written about Tiegerman in a memoir of Cairo life in "Cairo Recalled:
Growing Up in the Cultural Crosscurrents of 1940s Egypt," *House and Garden*, April
1987, pp. 20–32.
9. The clearest exposition of these ideas is found in Williams's *Politics and
Letters: Interviews with New Left Review.*(London: New Left Books, 1979), pp. 158–
74.

professional expertise itself depends to a degree on the knowledge that informs the structure of feeling I am discussing. I have long understood Tiegerman as suggesting that as one lives with music both practically and knowledgeably over time, one hears a composer's work—or for that matter any extended body of music—in more ways than those provided within the individual work's discrete boundaries. To listen to or play a piece by Brahms is also to summon one's prior acquaintance with, say, Beethoven and Schumann to the task, along with experience of ballades, variations, rondos, and rhapsodies generally, as well as other musical forms. Into this "hearing" of a composer there enter many components, all of them communicated and maintained as a sort of lore that in the end is internalized by the musician who plays, or for that matter by the listeners to, a work by a given composer. In other words, all the consolidations I talked about earlier are interdependent and disciplined, yet all of them require a mold or identity, ultimately solitary (but paradoxically social, that is, existing in a society or culture), that maintains Brahms as Brahms, Beethoven as Beethoven, Elliott Carter as Elliott Carter, and so on.

In *Contre Sainte-Beuve* Proust speaks of going beneath the surface of a book in order to distinguish there "the melody (*air de la chanson*) which in each author is different from the ones to be found in all other authors and, while I was reading, without being aware of it, I found myself singing to myself, I rushed or slowed the words or I interrupted them completely, in the way that one often sings or listens in time to a tune, before actually articulating the last part of a word."[10] These sentiments beautifully characterize the ultimately solitary intimacy by which the special music of an author impresses itself upon a receptive critical intelligence. The closest English equivalents to Proust's phrase *air de la chanson* are "tune" or "melody," so I think Proust means that he hears a writer's unique sound not only as a distinctive imprint, something like a signature or stamp of

10. Proust, *Contre Saint-Beuve* (Paris: Gallimard, 1971), p. 303.

particular possession, but also as a special theme, personal obsession, or recurrent motif in the work of an artist that gives all of his work its own recognizable identity. Later, in a famous series of observations, Proust says that the principle of art is personal, individual, original; books, he adds, are the work of solitude and the children of solitude ("l'oeuvre de la solitude et les *enfants du silence*"). On the other hand, the children of speech (*la parole*), with which literature has little in common, derives from the desire to say something, for instance, an opinion.[11]

I have always thought of Proust's comments as having application of a very rich kind to the musical experience. In speaking about the train of thoughts provoked by the Brahms Sextet variations I found myself finally coming to a sort of unstatable, or inexpressible, aspect of his music, the music of his music, which I think anyone who listens to, plays, or thinks about music carries within oneself. To extend the notion a bit further we could say that composers carry such a music within themselves too, although the case for an idea of that sort has been made only here and there in writing about music. I'll return to this in a moment when I take up two or three unusual instances of composers who seem quite consciously to be trying to state, as it were, the music of their music in their last compositions: Beethoven, Bruckner, Richard Strauss.

The point I want to make here is that all of this is conditional on a number of other circumstances that I shall now try to make explicit. First, both the metaphorical and the literal aspects of Proust's discussions of music depend not only on tonal music for their force but also on the melodic element in that music. Even if these things are granted, I think it probable that not all tonal music is served by Proust's figures: what does one do about complex late romantic composers like Mahler, who is principally tonal, but whose *air de la chanson* is a combination of things, drawn from *Ländler*, waltzes, fanfares, marches, etc.?

11. *Ibid.*, p. 309.

On the other hand, I believe melody itself is an expandable notion and was probably not intended to exclude, but rather to include, all those things that go into making up the particular idiom, or aesthetic statement, of composers or even of styles. Charles Rosen's assumption is that classical style as he analyzes it furnishes just the sort of distillation that could be called the melody of musical classicism in the Proustian sense. Similarly Wilfrid Mellers's studies, *Bach and the Dance of God* and *Beethoven and the Voice of God*, go the same way, although the focus is on individual composers. Both Mellers and Rosen, however, suggest that there is no quick route to these paradigmatic and quintessential melodies: tireless analysis of many examples is indispensable and an absolute requirement.

On the other hand, within the tonal universe as constituted by Western classical music until the early twentieth century melody itself does play a more and more prominent role as one traverses the whole territory, especially in the nineteenth century, but also earlier. Opera writing in the *opera seria, bel canto,* and *verismo* traditions is clearly a case in point, as is *lieder* composition. And of course in all our interactions with nineteenth-century music we do find ourselves saying of a piece by Schumann or Beethoven that its melody is typical of its author in his effort to refine and even strain after a central melodic utterance that conveys or expresses a particularly urgent mood unique to him. Vladimir Jankélévitch's *Fauré et l'inexprimable* is perhaps the most impressive effort to carry out such an analysis of one composer's work, but perhaps the main reason for its success is that Jankélévitch writes principally as an acute essayist and aetheticist, not as a musicologist whose scientific aims are very different indeed.

Here one is obliged to fall back upon characterizations that are fundamentally private, that derive with regard to a given composer from experiences of his/her music in a domain that is personal, self-enclosed, unprovable. In terms of melody, for instance, there is something about Schumann's *Widmung,* the Romance in F-sharp Major, and the first and third movements of the Second Symphony that to me represents the soulful, gently aggressive and affirmative, proclamatory, and yet reflective and poignant identity that stamps all of Schumann's work.

Similarly in the return of the main melody of Beethoven's *An die ferne geliebte*, in its striving sentimentality, in its heavily falling rhetorical cadence, a great deal is told me about the powerfully sentimental melodic core that Beethoven's forceful developments and formal innovations were frequently intended to discipline and school.

Adorno was right to insist upon the dictatorial character of Schoenberg's method, whose design was totally to replace the (to him) depleted and outworn capacities of conventional tonal music, with melody at its center. Wagner and Debussy played paramount roles in hastening the shifts from one organizational and aural regime to the other. The music that derives from the great modern Viennese revolution therefore displaces melody as conventionally understood, and highlights other elements, such as timbre, pitch, series, placement, all of which dictate a rather different aesthetic reception on the part of audience and performer alike. Still, I think, whether or not we listen to it differently as Adorno argued that we should, much twentieth-century music does try for effects of recognizable identity in which the notion of melody as authorial signature is still quite serviceable. Whether we hear it in Schoenberg's overwhelmingly powerful organizational and expressive drives in the fabric of the Piano Concerto, *Moses und Aron*, or the later piano pieces, or in Webern's ultimate compression in a pointillism of almost pure essence, or in Berg's wonderfully resourceful and programmatically nostalgic habit of combining heterogeneous styles for theatrical poignancy (nowhere with more success I think than in the adagio of the Violin Concerto)—the underlying and shaping compositional impulse is, indeed must be, registered by the interpreter with much the same force as in nineteenth century works. To the extent that the evolution of musical language and ambition comes out of the earlier classical tradition, the fundamental melodic identity of each composer's style keeps coming back, sometimes with overwhelmingly pleasurable force, as, for example, in the monumental and yet strangely delicate sound of Olivier Messiaen's music.

Let the word "melody" as I have discussed it from Proust therefore serve as a name both for an actual melody and for any other musical element that acts in or beneath the lines of a particular body of music to attach that music to the privacy of the listener's, performer's, or composer's experience. Here I want to emphasize privacy and pleasure, both of them replete with the historical and ideological residue of that bourgeois individuation now either discredited or fully under attack.

I come therefore to the second set of circumstances that condition the argument I have been presenting here. As we have gradually worked our way from the public to the private, can we locate the site of the solitary and highly individualized experiences with music that these various affirmations of melody entail? No one would want to gainsay or minimize the unattractive circumstances in which classical music exists today. As I said in Chapter One, Adorno spoke correctly of regressive hearing to underline the demotion of music to commodity status in contemporary society. Most people today are no longer amateur musicians, their knowledge of a musical work itself is sketchy and incomplete, there is continuous noise pollution all around, the mechanical means of reproducing music have multiplied unimaginably, and the music business, as it is usually called, includes (depending on where you look for its manifestations) extreme hermetic academism, commodified and commercialized record and concert packaging that privileges stars and superstars, and a constant "backgroundization" of music, from supermarket and elevator music, to commercial advertising, to the ceaseless hum of unattended, usually unacknowledged habitual sound emissions in daily life, through film, radio, television, Muzak, etc.

What is impressive is how persistently musicology and professional musicians call attention to the specialization in what they do. This is certainly an understandable position to take against the indiscriminate interventions and plunderings by the ordinary world upon the province of classical music. Defensive specialization is an ideological choice, however, but it is not the only choice, nor the only problem. Boulez's essays constantly call for dismissing, among other things, the ethnocentrism of the defensive attitude. Once we take for granted that classical music exists, and has always existed, among many competing cultural formations, affiliated with or disjunct from some or identical with others, we should be able to see how musical elaboration itself—the composition and performance of music —is an activity in civil society and is in overlapping, interdependent relationship with other activities. For Boulez, Messiaen furnishes an excellent instance of a distinctively daring paradigm, the musician whose resolute eclecticism frees him from the orthodoxies, traditions, and authorities in music whose main role is to keep things out, rather than to think things through together, heterophonically, variationally.[12]

The vulgarizations and repressions of which Adorno so often speaks are *consequences* of his theory of music, whose singular apartness and exilic distinctiveness in a society so given over to control provide its practioners and adherents (like Adorno) with fortitude and spiritual strength. In fact, music has always taken place, so to speak, in mixed public and private circumstances. None of us is involved in music to the exclusion of other things, and it has been no small achievement of one of Adorno's most gifted and independent admirers, Pierre Boulez, to have driven the point home repeatedly in his essays and treatises: serious musical thought occurs in conjunction with, not in separation from, other serious thought, both musical *and* nonmusical. This insight helps me to note that my Brahms variations experiences are themselves threaded through with earlier as well as contemporary, with other Western as well as non-Western, musics—for example, the singing of Umm Kalthoum with which I grew up, rock and jazz, the hymns and folk-songs I also grew up with, and so forth.

What I find interesting here is how many of my own earlier

12. Pierre Boulez, *Orientations: Collected Writings*, ed. Martin Cooper (London: Faber and Faber, 1986), pp. 406–7.

musical experiences persist and keep returning, despite my conscious feelings that they have either been superseded by substantial changes in my taste or forgotten and left behind in a past with which I no longer have an active connection. The first musical performance I ever attended as a very small boy (in the mid-1940s) was a puzzling, interminably long, and yet haunting concert by Umm Kalthoum, already the premier exponent of classical Arabic song. I had no way of knowing that her peculiar rigor as performer derived from an aesthetic whose hallmark was exfoliating variation, in which repetition, a sort of meditative fixation on one or two small patterns, and an almost total absence of developmental (in the Beethovenian sense) tension were the key elements. The point of the performance, I later realized, was not to get to the end of a carefully constructed logical structure—working through it—but to luxuriate in all sorts of byways, to linger over details and changes in text, to digress and then digress from the digression. And because, in my preponderantly Western education (both musical and academic) I seemed to be dedicated to an ethic of productivity and of overcoming obstacles, the kind of art practiced by Umm Kalthoum receded in importance for me. But of course it only went beneath the surface of my conscious awareness until, in recent years, I returned to an interest in Arabic culture, where I rediscovered her, and was able to associate what she did musically with some features of Western classical music.

The consolidations and affirmations I described as belonging to the relative solitude of the private sphere are enabled and empowered by certain aspects of what exists for everyone in the public sphere. By public sphere I mean something looser than what Jürgen Habermas analyzes as *Offentlichkeit;* I mean simply what is available to anyone by virtue of historical experience and by membership in a society and culture. To think of those realities as constraints or limitations is certainly correct— but only up to a point, for otherwise we would risk getting trapped in the apocalyptic determinisms of which I wrote earlier. To think of the public sphere, so far as music is concerned, as also containing alternative and emergent formations, not just the enforceable but extremely challengeable norms promulgated ideologically in certain classical musical practices, is no less important an exercise. Messaien's aesthetic seems absolutely crucial here as a sort of symbol of the alternative: I refer to both his discursively expressed ideas and his music itself as an attempt to realize the ideas. To summarize the relevant points: whereas the main Western musical tradition by and large relies upon development, control, inventiveness, and rhythm in the service of forward logical control, Messaien's music is consciously at some eccentric distance from these characteristics. Instead his work emphasizes repetition and stasis. His harmonies, as Paul Griffiths says in his essential book on Messaien, are "objects of contemplation, not subjects of action."[13] He cares neither for the strictly centralized rigor of polyphony—heterophony is what he employs—nor for the attitude to time that stresses its march forward. Much in these notions can be directly traced to Messiaen's openly stated religious views—his adoration of God, his inexhaustible attention to mystery, his untiring interest in the correspondence between modal and natural patterns (birdsongs, most famously).

Messaien in short is an anti- or non-narrative alternative to the mainstream tradition, which the divagations of his music do a lot to hold up and even out. Yet his piety and his inventiveness have, perhaps ironically, sought the widest public acknowledgments. Few composers write more demandingly for performer, audience, or concert-hall managers; and yet few contemporary composers are as performed and as (evidently) enjoyed by a wide public as he. None of his music that I know fails to produce remarkable pleasures, admittedly local and not theological (for staunch secularists like myself) but always musical and intelligent. The point I am trying to make is that Proust's talking about the distinctive *air de la chanson* of each

13. Paul Griffiths, *Messiaen and the Music of Time* (London: Faber and Faber, 1985), p. 15.

original artist and Messiaen's antinarrative aesthetic are styles of diverting and prying us away from the principal discursive stands that mainstream classical music embodies and carries forward. From one perspective, music in the great Austro-Germanic classic tradition represents for them the complete coincidence between aesthetic and sociohistorical time: this is music available and experienceable as coeval with the history that produced it. From the different, private perspective of a contrary artist, however, music is another way of telling (in John Berger's eminently valid phrase), digressive, reiterative, slower in its effects because built up through the whole series of affirmations and associations that come with not focusing on getting through time but of being *in* time, experiencing it together, rather than in competition, with other musics, experiences, temporalities.

Looked at even more closely these examples of a countertradition in Western and non-Western classical music are saved from sentimentality by the critical force of that tradition itself. So much of the discipline of music is severe and rigorous, so much of it dominative and specialized—the two qualities so clearly reinforcing each other—that it is no wonder that sonata form, which can be read and is frequently described as a disciplinary essentialization of coercive development, achieved so great an authority in classical ninteenth century compositional and performance techniques. The model for the sonata form, is, I think, pedagogic and dramatic: what we have in it is the demonstration of authoritative control in which a thematic statement and its subsequent development are worked through rigorously by the composer. Where? In the space opened up between two strongly marked poles, the inaugural declarations, which is where the theme first gets stated, and at the end, which is where a final cadential formula winds things up.

Thus themes undergo development, there is a calculated alternation between dominant and tonic keys, and a clangorous affirmation of the composer's authority over his material is achieved. Some of the excesses of romantic music are clear attempts to play with this astringent pattern, although quite often (in Liszt, Chopin, Schumann, and Mendelssohn) the pattern seems either to ensnare or to haunt the incautious and unconsciously programmed romantic explorer who has internalized the sonata script as part of his musical literacy. An interesting yet relatively early case of attempted break with the pattern is the third-period Beethoven, for whom a fascination with both fugal and variational forms (for example, opus 106, the *Diabelli* Variations) is his way of getting away from the coerciveness of sonata form, opening music out exfoliatively, elaborately, contemplatively.

At the risk of caricatural simplification I find myself speculating finally that two of the main organizational tendencies in Western classical music derive from two different ways of looking at theme, melody, or statement. Looked at horizontally, statement is melody, to be pronounced robustly, carefully developed, definitively ended. This is mastering time according to a linear model, working through the material strictly. Looked at nonnarratively, however, music is not just statement, but statement and infinitely possible variations, not just, for example, the variations written by Brahms that I discussed earlier (elaborations of the form that Walter Frisch has called Brahms's developing variations)[14] but the variations in the use to which I found myself privately putting them. These uses need not always be contemplative, but in the case of a contemporary set of theme and variations that I greatly admire, they can be political, open, even noisy. I refer here to Frederic Rzewski's extraordinary piano variations on "The People United Will Never Be defeated!"

Perhaps all I am saying is that in my experience of music the composer's *air de la chanson* I hold onto and whose embellishments over time I enjoy represents a personal obsession of the individual hearer or interpreter, with no more status than those pathetic family photographs described by Berger as "fragile

14. See Walter Frisch, *Brahms and the Principles of Developing Variation* (Berkeley: University of California Press, 1984).

images, often carried next to the heart or placed by the side of the bed . . . used to refer to that which historical time has no right to destroy." [15] Perhaps. But I am intellectually impressed by the richness of what I have called the alternative formation in music, in which the nonlinear, nondevelopmental uses of theme or melody dissipate and delay a disciplined organization of musical time that is principally combative as well as dominative. Glenn Gould, I think, understood the potential interest in this essentially contrapuntal mode—that is, you think of and treat one musical line in conjunction with several others that derive from and relate to it, and you do so through imitation, repetition, or ornamentation—as an antidote to the more overtly administrative and executive authority contained in, say, a Mozart or Beethoven classical sonata form.

Obviously I'm *not* saying that classical forms like the sonata are neurotically un-beautiful. That would be nonsense. But I am proposing that one can think about musical elaboration as something to be returned to for reasons other than its finished perfection, that the essence of the elaboration can be transformative and reflective, that it can occur slowly not only because we affirm and reaffirm its repetition, its meandering course, but also because it too seems to be about the same process, the way, for example, there is something both reflective and circular—without regard for impressive development—in the leisurely, majestic unfolding of Bruckner's Ninth Symphony (Example 17).

I do not think it is an accident that the one major twentieth-century composer who intransigently (some would say heedlessly and irresponsibly) followed his own studiously self-devised path despite the innumerable opportunities offered him by serialism, neoclassicism, nationalism, etc., is Richard Strauss. In his last years, significantly enough, Strauss turned almost exclusively to various quite extraordinary transfigurations of

15. John Berger, *Another Way of Telling*, with photographs by Jean Mohr (New York: Pantheon, 1982), p. 108.

EXAMPLE 17. Bruckner, Symphony No. 9

the variation idea. Consider the Oboe Concerto, *Capriccio*, the Four Last Songs, and, most remarkably of all, *Metamorphosen*, an essay in almost pure repetition and contemplation. Each of this handful of works is poignantly summational, as if Strauss had been trying to recapitulate the ethos of his craft in various musical genres—orchestral, vocal, operatic, chamber ensembles. But the overall effect is of a magisterial narrowing of focus, and with it a deepening of scrutiny, so that measure by measure he allowed himself to repeat an earlier idea but also to vary it almost microscopically. Thus the effect is of a lateral movement outward, expanding slowly and contemplatively, in the case of *Metamorphosen* using a text taken from the second movement of Beethoven's *Eroica* as the thematic starting point for the unfolding variations. That the occasion is a mournful and even funereal one only adds to the work's majestically slow and inward self-contemplation (Example 18).

But I would be incomplete here if I did not mention that Strauss's late style is often quite deliberately elegiac (understandably so for a grieving man in his eighties). The reiterative variational techniques are sustained by a conscious affirmation of how musical time can become the subject of a musical treatment more concerned with its own internal complexities than with dramatic control. Glenn Gould calls Strauss's work gener-

EXAMPLE 18. Richard Strauss, *Metamorphosen*

ally ecstatic,[16] but in the context of what I have been discussing here, it is, I believe, radically, beautifully elaborative, music whose pleasures and discoveries are premised upon letting go, upon not asserting a central authorizing identity, upon enlarging the community of hearers and players beyond the time taken, beyond the extremely concentrated duration provided by the performance occasion. In the perspective afforded by such a work as *Metamorphosen*, music thus becomes an art not primarily or exclusively about authorial power and social authority, but a mode for thinking through or thinking with the integral variety of human cultural practices, generously, non-coercively, and, yes, in a utopian cast, if by utopian we mean worldly, possible, attainable, knowable.

16. *The Glenn Gould Reader*, ed. Tim Page (New York: Alfred A. Knopf, 1984), p. 91.

# Index